ESSENTIAL AIR FRYER RECIPES

Publications International, Ltd.

Louis Weber, CEO
Publications International, Ltd.
8140 Lehigh Ave
Morton Grove, IL 60053

Pictured on the front cover *(clockwise from left):* Soy Ginger Salmon *(page 115),* Air-Fried Green Beans *(page 174)* and Open-Faced Steak and Blue Cheese Sandwiches *(page 84).*

Pictured on the back cover *(clockwise from top):* Strawberry Banana French Toast *(page 12),* Supersize Shrimp *(page 134),* Steak and Mushroom Supper *(page 80)* and Loaded Tater Tots *(page 44).*

ISBN: 978-1-63938-830-1

Manufactured in China.

8 7 6 5 4 3 2 1

Microwave Cooking: Microwave ovens vary in wattage. Use the cooking times as guidelines and check for doneness before adding more time.

WARNING: Food preparation, baking and cooking involve inherent dangers: misuse of electric products, sharp electric tools, boiling water, hot stoves, allergic reactions, foodborne illnesses and the like, pose numerous potential risks. Publications International, Ltd. (PIL) assumes no responsibility or liability for any damages you may experience as a result of following recipes, instructions, tips or advice in this publication.

While we hope this publication helps you find new ways to eat delicious foods, you may not always achieve the results desired due to variations in ingredients, cooking temperatures, typos, errors, omissions or individual cooking abilities.

CONTENTS

INTRODUCTION

It seems like everyone is air frying these days—with good reason! The air fryer not only makes delicious, crispy, crunchy—and often healthier—food, but it also makes everyday cooking quicker and easier.

Now you can find the essential air fryer recipes all in one place—more than 95 recipes for family-pleasing meals that don't require hours of prep or clean-up time. Use your air fryer for a wide variety of dishes, including appetizers, snacks, sandwiches, vegetables and so much more. Quesadillas and tater tots are two of the easiest and all-time favorite air fryer options. Spicy wings, crispy fries and chicken tenders are guaranteed crowd pleasers you can make with minimal time and mess. Try flatbreads or frittatas for quick-to-fix lunches, or cook juicy burgers, chicken, steak and pork chop dinners in no time—they're all easier with an air fryer!

Helpful Tips

- Read the manufacturer's directions for your air fryer carefully before cooking to make sure you understand the specific settings and features of your machine.
- Preheat your air fryer for 2 to 3 minutes before cooking.
- To avoid foods sticking to your air fryer basket, use nonstick cooking spray or cook on parchment paper or foil. Spraying food occasionally with nonstick cooking spray during the cooking process will also help food to brown and crisp more easily.
- Don't overfill your basket. Smaller air fryers may require cooking food in several batches. Some foods should be cooked in a single layer for best results (as noted in the recipes), so cook these items in batches as needed. Crowding the basket will prevent foods from crisping and browning evenly.
- Use toothpicks to hold food in place. Sometimes light foods may blow around from the pressure of the fan, such as the top of a quesadilla or the top slice of bread in a sandwich. Securing foods in the basket with toothpicks can prevent this from happening.
- Check foods during cooking and turn the food or shake the basket for even browning, if necessary. This will not affect cooking times—once you return the basket, the cooking (and the timing) resumes.

- Experiment with cooking times of various foods, as different models of air fryers may cook slightly faster and cooking times can vary. Test foods for doneness before serving them; check meats and poultry with a meat thermometer, and use a toothpick to test muffins and cupcakes.
- Use a foil sling to get cake pans or baking dishes in and out of the air fryer basket. Fold a 24-inch piece of foil into a 2-inch-wide strip; place the pan in the center and use the ends to hold and raise or lower the dish into the air fryer. Tuck the ends down while cooking so the drawer can close.
- You can use your air fryer to cook foods typically prepared in the oven. But because the air fryer is more condensed than a regular oven, it is recommended that you reduce the temperature by 25°F to 50°F and reduce the cooking time by 20 percent when converting standard oven recipes to the air fryer.
- Use your air fryer to cook frozen foods, too! Frozen French fries, fish sticks, chicken nuggets, individual pizzas—these all work wonderfully in the air fryer. Just remember to reduce the cooking temperatures and times as recommended above.

Estimated Cooking Temperatures/Times*

FOOD	TEMPERATURE	TIMING
Beef (ground beef)	370°F	15 to 17 minutes
Beef (steaks)	390°F	10 to 15 minutes
Chicken (bone-in)	370°F	20 to 25 minutes
Chicken (boneless)	370°F	12 to 15 minutes
Fish	390°F	10 to 12 minutes
Frozen Foods	390°F	10 to 15 minutes
Pork	370°F	12 to 15 minutes
Vegetables (asparagus, broccoli, corn on the cob, green beans, mushrooms, tomatoes)	390°F	6 to 10 minutes
Vegetables (bell peppers, cauliflower, eggplant, onions, potatoes, zucchini)	390°F	10 to 15 minutes

**These times are a general guide. Foods vary in size, weight and texture—and different air fryers cook at different rates—so be sure to test your food for doneness before consuming it. For best results, some foods need to be shaken or turned during cooking.*

BREAKFAST

Jelly-Filled Doughnuts

MAKES 20 DOUGHNUTS

- **1 package (about 7 ounces) refrigerated biscuit dough (10 biscuits)**
- **¼ cup coarse sugar**
- **1 cup strawberry preserves***

**If preserves are very chunky, process in food processor 10 seconds or press through fine-mesh sieve.*

1. Separate biscuits. Cut each biscuit in half; roll dough into balls to create 20 balls.
2. Place sugar in large bowl. Preheat air fryer to 370°F. Spray dough balls with nonstick cooking spray.
3. Cook in batches 5 to 6 minutes or until golden brown, shaking occasionally and spraying with cooking spray.
4. Roll warm doughnuts in sugar to coat.
5. Fit piping bag with medium round or star tip; fill bag with preserves. Poke hole in side of each doughnut with paring knife; fill with preserves. Serve immediately.

Mini Spinach Frittatas

MAKES 6 MINI FRITTATAS

6 eggs
2 tablespoons milk
¾ cup thawed frozen chopped spinach, squeezed dry
¼ cup shredded white Cheddar cheese
¼ cup grated Parmesan cheese
1 teaspoon dried minced onion
½ teaspoon salt
⅛ teaspoon black pepper
Pinch ground red pepper
Pinch ground nutmeg

1 Preheat air fryer to 330°F. Spray six (4-ounce) ramekins* with nonstick cooking spray.

2 Beat eggs and milk in large bowl until well blended. Stir in spinach, Cheddar, Parmesan, dried onion, salt, black pepper, red pepper and nutmeg. Divide mixture evenly among ramekins.

3 Cook 12 minutes or until eggs are puffed and firm and no longer shiny. (Cook in batches if necessary.) Cool 5 minutes.

4 Loosen bottom and sides with small spatula or knife; remove to wire rack. Serve warm or at room temperature.

**Or use a 6-cup standard muffin pan if this fits in your air fryer; spray pan with nonstick cooking spray.*

Strawberry Banana French Toast

MAKES 2 SERVINGS

- 1 cup sliced fresh strawberries (about 8 medium)
- 2 teaspoons granulated sugar
- 2 eggs
- ½ cup milk
- 3 tablespoons all-purpose flour
- 1 teaspoon vanilla
- ⅛ teaspoon salt
- 4 slices (1 inch thick) egg bread or country bread
- 1 banana, cut into ¼-inch slices
- Whipped cream and powdered sugar (optional)
- Maple syrup

1. Combine strawberries and granulated sugar in small bowl; toss to coat. Set aside while preparing French toast.
2. Whisk eggs, milk, flour, vanilla and salt in shallow dish or pie plate until well blended. Working with two slices at a time, dip bread into egg mixture, turning to coat completely and letting excess drip back into dish.
3. Preheat air fryer to 370°F.
4. Cook bread in batches 8 to 10 minutes or until golden brown.
5. Top each serving with strawberry mixture and banana slices. Garnish with whipped cream and powdered sugar, if desired. Serve with maple syrup.

Air-Fried Omelet Scramble

MAKES 2 SERVINGS

- 2 large eggs
- 2 tablespoons milk
- ¼ teaspoon salt
- ⅛ teaspoon black pepper
- 2 tablespoons chopped red and/or green bell pepper
- 2 tablespoons chopped onion
- ¼ cup (1 ounce) shredded Cheddar cheese, divided

1. Spray 6×3-inch baking dish or 2 small ramekins* with nonstick cooking spray.
2. Beat eggs, milk, salt and black pepper in medium bowl until well blended. Stir in bell pepper, onion and 2 tablespoons cheese. Pour into prepared baking dish.
3. Preheat air fryer to 350°F.
4. Cook 10 to 12 minutes, slightly breaking up eggs after 5 minutes. Top with remaining 2 tablespoons cheese.

**Depending on the size of your air fryer, you may need to modify size of baking dish.*

Ricotta Pancakes

MAKES 8 TO 10 PANCAKES

- 1 container (15 ounces) whole milk ricotta cheese
- 1 egg
- ½ teaspoon vanilla
- ¼ cup granulated sugar
- 1 cup all-purpose flour, divided
- ¼ teaspoon baking powder
- ½ cup seedless raspberry jam
- Powdered sugar
- Fresh raspberries (optional)

1. Whisk ricotta, egg and vanilla in large bowl until blended. Add granulated sugar, ¾ cup flour and baking powder; whisk until blended. Place remaining ¼ cup flour in shallow dish.
2. Scoop about ¼ to ½ cup ricotta mixture into a ball. Add to bowl with flour; turn to coat. Flatten into pancake about ½ inch thick. Repeat with remaining batter. Spray pancakes with nonstick cooking spray.
3. Preheat air fryer to 370°F. Line basket with parchment paper.
4. Cook pancakes in batches 14 to 16 minutes or until lightly browned, turning and spraying with cooking spray after 10 minutes.
5. Place jam in small microwavable bowl; microwave on HIGH 30 seconds or until melted. Drizzle over warm pancakes; sprinkle with powdered sugar. Top with raspberries, if desired.

Spinach and Egg Quesadillas

MAKES 2 SERVINGS

- ¼ teaspoon salt, divided
- 1 plum tomato, diced
- 2 eggs
- ⅛ teaspoon black pepper
- 1 teaspoon vegetable oil or butter
- 4 (6-inch) flour tortillas
- ½ cup (2 ounces) grated Monterey Jack cheese
- 1 cup baby spinach
- 1 green onion, finely chopped
- ¼ cup crumbled feta or goat cheese
- Sour cream, salsa and/or hot pepper sauce (optional)

1 Sprinkle ⅛ teaspoon salt over tomato in small bowl; stir to blend. Set aside. Beat eggs, remaining ⅛ teaspoon salt and pepper in medium bowl.

2 Heat oil in small nonstick skillet over medium heat. Add egg mixture; cook without stirring 1 minute. Cook 2 to 3 minutes or just until eggs are softly set but not dry, stirring frequently. Remove to plate.

3 Place two tortillas on work surface. Sprinkle each with 2 tablespoons Monterey Jack; top with ½ cup spinach and half of scrambled eggs. Sprinkle with half of tomato, half of green onion, remaining Monterey Jack and feta. Top with remaining tortillas.

4 Preheat air fryer to 350°F. Spray basket with nonstick cooking spray. Place one quesadilla in basket; spray with cooking spray. Place metal trivet, measuring cup or dinner knife on top of quesadilla (to prevent top tortilla from blowing off).

5 Cook 4 minutes; turn and cook 2 to 3 minutes or until lightly browned. Repeat with remaining quesadilla. Cut into quarters; serve with sour cream, if desired.

Crunchy French Toast

MAKES 4 SERVINGS

2 cups wheat and barley flakes or corn flakes cereal

¾ teaspoon ground cinnamon, divided

4 eggs

1 cup milk

1 tablespoon sugar

1 teaspoon vanilla

8 slices whole wheat, white or cinnamon raisin bread

Stawberry fruit topping and/or maple syrup

1 Place cereal in large resealable food storage bag. Seal bag; crush cereal into coarse crumbs with rolling pin or meat mallet. Transfer to shallow dish; stir in ¼ teaspoon cinnamon.

2 Beat eggs, milk, sugar, vanilla and remaining ½ teaspoon cinnamon in another shallow dish until well blended. Cut bread slices diagonally in half.

3 Preheat air fryer to 370°F. Spray basket with nonstick cooking spray.

4 Working with one at a time, dip bread slices in egg mixture, turning to coat completely and letting excess drip back into dish. Place in dish of cereal crumbs; turn to coat. Arrange in single layer in basket, making sure slices do not touch.

5 Cook in batches 5 minutes; turn and cook 3 minutes or until golden brown. Serve with desired toppngs.

Mini Broccoli Frittatas

MAKES 4 SERVINGS

- 1 small broccoli crown (about 4 ounces)
- 1 tablespoon olive oil
- ¼ cup chopped red onion
- 2 tablespoons water
- ½ teaspoon salt, divided
- 2 tablespoons chopped roasted red pepper
- Pinch red pepper flakes
- ¼ cup crumbled goat or feta cheese
- 4 eggs
- 2 tablespoons grated Parmesan or Asiago cheese
- 2 tablespoons chopped fresh basil *or* ½ teaspoon dried basil
- ¼ teaspoon black pepper

1. Peel off tough outer skin of broccoli stem with paring knife; chop stem into ¼-inch pieces. Chop top of broccoli into small florets (about ½ inch).
2. Heat oil in large skillet over medium-high heat. Add onion; cook and stir 2 minutes. Add broccoli, 2 tablespoons water and ¼ teaspoon salt; cook and stir about 5 minutes or until broccoli is crisp-tender. Add roasted pepper and red pepper flakes; cook and stir 1 minute. Remove vegetables to small bowl; stir in goat cheese.
3. Preheat air fryer to 330°F. Spray four (4-ounce) ramekins with nonstick cooking spray.
4. Beat eggs, Parmesan, basil, remaining ¼ teaspoon salt and black pepper in medium bowl until well blended. Divide vegetable mixture evenly among prepared ramekins; pour egg mixture over vegetables.
5. Cook frittatas 15 to 18 minutes or until toothpick inserted into centers comes out clean. Cool 5 minutes. Serve in ramekins or run small knife or spatula around edges to loosen and turn out onto plates.

Homemade Air-Fried Bagels

MAKES 4 SERVINGS

1 cup self-rising flour
1 cup plain Greek yogurt
1 egg, beaten
Sesame seeds, poppy seeds, dried onion flakes, everything bagel seasoning (optional)

1. Combine flour and yogurt in bowl of stand mixer;* mix with dough hook at medium speed 2 to 3 minutes or until well blended.
2. Turn out dough onto lightly floured surface; knead 4 to 5 minutes or until dough is smooth and elastic.
3. Shape dough into a ball. Cut dough into four pieces; roll each piece into a ball. Pull and stretch dough to create round bagel shape, inserting finger into center to create hole.
4. Preheat air fryer to 330°F. Line basket with parchment paper.
5. Place bagels in single layer in basket; brush with egg and sprinkle with desired toppings.
6. Cook bagels 8 to 10 minutes or until lightly browned.

**Or use heavy spatula to mix dough in large bowl.*

Omelet Croissants

MAKES 2 SERVINGS

- 2 large croissants
- 2 eggs
- ¼ cup chopped mushrooms
- 1 tablespoon chopped red and/or green bell pepper
- Pinch of salt and black pepper
- ¼ cup (1 ounce) shredded Cheddar cheese

1. Cut lengthwise slit across top of each croissant. Use hands to break open croissants and pull apart slightly to create space for eggs.
2. Beat eggs in medium bowl; stir in mushrooms, bell pepper, salt and black pepper. Spoon mixture into croissant openings; sprinkle with cheese.
3. Preheat air fryer to 330°F. Line basket with parchment paper.
4. Cook 12 to 15 minutes or until eggs are set and croissants are lightly browned.

STARTERS & SNACKS

Pigs in a Blanket

MAKES 6 TO 8 SERVINGS

1 package (8 ounces) refrigerated crescent roll dough
24 cocktail franks (one 10- to 12-ounce package)
Mustard (optional)

1 Unroll dough on cutting board or work surface; separate into eight triangles. Cut each triangle into three long, thin triangles.

2 Place one frank at base of each triangle; roll up toward opposite point. Wrap strip of dough around each frank.

3 Preheat air fryer to 350°F.

4 Cook in batches 3 to 4 minutes or until golden brown. Serve with mustard, if desired.

Jalapeño Poppers

MAKES 20 POPPERS

- 10 medium jalapeño peppers
- 1 package (8 ounces) cream cheese, softened
- 1½ cups (6 ounces) shredded Cheddar cheese, divided
- 2 green onions, finely chopped
- ½ teaspoon onion powder
- ¼ teaspoon salt
- ⅛ teaspoon garlic powder
- 6 slices bacon, crisp-cooked and crumbled* *or* 2 tablespoons bacon bits
- 2 tablespoons panko bread crumbs
- 2 tablespoons grated Parmesan or Romano cheese

**Cook bacon in preheated 390°F air fryer 6 to 8 minutes or until crisp. Remove to paper towel-lined plate to drain.*

1 Cut each jalapeño pepper in half lengthwise; remove ribs and seeds.

2 Combine cream cheese, 1 cup Cheddar, green onions, onion powder, salt and garlic powder in medium bowl; mix well. Stir in bacon.

3 Fill each pepper half with about 1 tablespoon cheese mixture. Sprinkle with remaining ½ cup Cheddar, panko and Parmesan.

4 Preheat air fryer to 370°F. Line basket with parchment paper or foil.

5 Cook 5 to 7 minutes or until cheese is melted and beginning to brown but peppers are still firm.

Toasted Tortellini

MAKES 6 TO 8 SERVINGS

- 2 eggs
- 2 tablespoons milk
- ⅔ cup Italian seasoned bread crumbs
- 1 teaspoon garlic powder
- 2 tablespoons grated Parmesan cheese
- ½ teaspoon salt
- 1 package (9 ounces) refrigerated tortellini
- Chopped fresh parsley
- Marinara sauce, warmed

1. Beat eggs and milk in shallow dish. Combine bread crumbs, garlic powder, cheese and salt in another shallow dish.
2. Dip tortellini in egg mixture, letting excess drip back into dish. Roll tortellini in bread crumb mixture to coat. Spray with nonstick cooking spray.
3. Preheat air fryer to 370°F. Spray basket with cooking spray.
4. Cook tortellini in single layer 6 to 8 minutes or until golden brown and crisp, shaking halfway through cooking. Sprinkle with parsley; serve with marinara sauce.

Asian Barbecue Skewers

MAKES 4 TO 6 SERVINGS

- ½ cup reduced-sodium soy sauce
- ⅓ cup packed brown sugar
- 2 tablespoons sesame oil
- 2 teaspoons garlic powder
- ⅛ teaspoon red pepper flakes (optional)
- 2 pounds boneless skinless chicken thighs, cut into 1-inch-wide strips
- 1 tablespoon barbecue sauce
- 1 tablespoon toasted sesame seeds (optional)

1. Combine soy sauce, brown sugar, oil, garlic powder and red pepper flakes, if desired, in medium bowl; mix well. Remove ⅓ cup mixture to small bowl; set aside.
2. Add chicken to remaining mixture; stir to coat. Cover and marinate 30 minutes or marinate up to 8 hours in refrigerator. Soak 16 (7-inch) wooden skewers in water 20 minutes to prevent burning.
3. Thread chicken onto skewers. Preheat air fryer to 370°F. Line basket with parchment paper.
4. Cook skewers in single layer 12 minutes or until chicken is cooked through, turning halfway through cooking.
5. Stir barbecue sauce into reserved soy sauce mixture; brush over skewers immediately after cooking. Sprinkle with sesame seeds, if desired.

Parmesan Pickle Chips

MAKES 8 SERVINGS

- 4 large whole dill pickles
- ½ cup all-purpose flour
- ½ teaspoon salt
- 2 eggs
- ½ cup panko bread crumbs
- 2 tablespoons grated Parmesan cheese
- Ranch dressing or garlic mayonnaise

1 Line baking sheet with paper towels. Cut pickles diagonally into ¼-inch slices; place on prepared baking sheet. Pat dry with paper towels to remove any moisture from pickles.

2 Combine flour and salt in shallow dish. Beat eggs in another shallow dish. Combine panko and cheese in third shallow dish.

3 Coat pickles with flour. Dip in eggs, letting excess drip back into dish, then roll in panko mixture to coat.

4 Preheat air fryer to 390°F.

5 Cook pickles in batches 8 to 10 minutes or until golden brown, shaking halfway through cooking. Serve with ranch dressing.

Buffalo Cauliflower Bites

MAKES 4 SERVINGS

- ½ cup all-purpose flour
- ½ cup water
- ½ teaspoon garlic powder
- ½ teaspoon salt
- ¼ teaspoon black pepper
- 1 small head cauliflower, cut into small florets
- 3 tablespoons hot pepper sauce
- 1 tablespoon melted butter
- Blue cheese dressing and celery sticks (optional)

1. Combine flour, water, garlic powder, salt and black pepper in large bowl; mix well. Add cauliflower; stir until well coated.
2. Preheat air fryer to 390°F. Line basket with parchment paper.
3. Cook cauliflower 12 to 15 minutes or until slightly tender and browned, shaking occasionally during cooking.
4. Meanwhile, combine hot pepper sauce and butter in medium bowl. Add warm cauliflower; toss to coat.
5. Serve with blue cheese dressing and celery, if desired.

Bruschetta

MAKES 8 SERVINGS

- 4 plum tomatoes, seeded and diced
- ½ cup packed fresh basil leaves, finely chopped
- 5 tablespoons olive oil, divided
- 2 cloves garlic, minced
- 2 teaspoons finely chopped oil-packed sun-dried tomatoes
- ¼ teaspoon salt
- ⅛ teaspoon black pepper
- 16 slices Italian bread
- 2 tablespoons grated Parmesan cheese

1. Combine fresh tomatoes, basil, 3 tablespoons oil, garlic, sun-dried tomatoes, salt and pepper in large bowl; mix well. Let stand at room temperature 1 hour to blend flavors.
2. Brush remaining 2 tablespoons oil over one side of bread slices; sprinkle with cheese.
3. Preheat air fryer to 350°F.
4. Cook bread slices in single layer 3 to 5 minutes or until toasted.
5. Top each bread slice with 1 tablespoon tomato mixture.

Crispy Mushrooms

MAKES 4 SERVINGS

MUSHROOMS

- ½ cup all-purpose flour
- ½ cup garlic and herb-flavored bread crumbs
- ½ cup grated Parmesan cheese
- ½ teaspoon paprika
- ½ teaspoon salt
- ¼ teaspoon black pepper
- 2 eggs
- 1 teaspoon water
- 1 package (8 ounces) whole mushrooms

GARLIC MAYONNAISE

- ½ cup mayonnaise
- 2 teaspoons minced garlic
- 1 teaspoon lemon juice
- Chopped fresh parsley (optional)

1 Combine flour, bread crumbs, cheese, paprika, salt and pepper in shallow dish. Beat eggs and water in another shallow dish.

2 Use fork to dip mushrooms into egg mixture, allowing excess to drip back into dish. Roll in bread crumb mixture to coat. Spray mushrooms with nonstick cooking spray.

3 Preheat air fryer to 370°F. Line basket with parchment paper.

4 Cook mushrooms in batches 6 to 8 minutes or until golden brown, shaking and spraying with cooking spray halfway through cooking.

5 Combine mayonnaise, garlic and lemon juice in small bowl; mix well. Sprinkle with parsley, if desired. Serve with mushrooms.

Loaded Tater Tots

MAKES 3 TO 4 SERVINGS

- 1 package (16 ounces) frozen bite-size potato nuggets (tater tots)
- ½ cup (2 ounces) shredded Cheddar cheese
- 2 slices bacon, crisp-cooked and crumbled* *or* 2 tablespoons bacon bits
- 2 tablespoons sour cream
- 2 green onions, chopped
- Chopped avocado (optional)

**Cook bacon in preheated 390°F air fryer 6 to 8 minutes or until crisp. Remove to paper towel-lined plate to drain.*

1. Preheat air fryer to 390°F.
2. Cook potatoes in single layer 6 to 8 minutes, shaking occasionally during cooking.
3. Transfer potatoes to baking dish that fits inside air fryer; sprinkle with cheese and bacon. Cook 2 to 3 minutes or until cheese is melted.
4. Drizzle with sour cream; sprinkle with green onions and avocado, if desired. Serve immediately.

Quick and Easy Arancini

MAKES 12 TO 15 ARANCINI

- **1 package (6 to 8 ounces) sun-dried tomato, mushroom or Milanese risotto mix, plus ingredients to prepare mix***
- **½ cup frozen peas *or* ¼ cup finely chopped oil-packed sun-dried tomatoes (optional)**
- **½ cup panko bread crumbs**
- **¼ cup finely shredded or grated Parmesan cheese**
- **2 tablespoons minced fresh parsley**
- **4 ounces Swiss, Asiago or fontina cheese, cut into 15 cubes (about ½ inch)**

Or use 3 cups leftover risotto.

1. Prepare risotto according to package directions. Stir in peas, if desired. Let stand, uncovered, 20 minutes or until thickened and cool enough to handle.
2. Combine panko, cheese and parsley in shallow dish. Shape ¼ cupfuls risotto into balls around Swiss cheese cubes, covering completely. Roll in panko mixture to coat.
3. Preheat air fryer to 370°F. Line basket with parchment paper; spray with nonstick cooking spray.
4. Place arancini in single layer in basket; spray with nonstick cooking spray.
5. Cook arancini 6 minutes; turn and spray with nonstick cooking spray. Cook 6 minutes or until lightly browned. Serve warm.

Falafel Nuggets

MAKES 12 SERVINGS

SAUCE

- 2½ cups tomato sauce
- ⅓ cup tomato paste
- 2 tablespoons lemon juice
- 2 teaspoons sugar
- 1 teaspoon onion powder
- ½ teaspoon salt

FALAFEL

- 2 cans (about 15 ounces each) chickpeas, rinsed and drained
- ½ cup all-purpose flour
- ½ cup chopped fresh parsley
- 1 egg
- ¼ cup minced onion
- 3 tablespoons lemon juice
- 2 tablespoons minced garlic
- 2 teaspoons ground cumin
- ½ teaspoon salt
- ¼ teaspoon ground red pepper or red pepper flakes

1. For sauce, combine tomato sauce, tomato paste, 2 tablespoons lemon juice, sugar, onion powder and ½ teaspoon salt in medium saucepan; simmer over medium-low heat 20 minutes. Cover and keep warm until ready to serve.
2. For falafel, combine chickpeas, flour, parsley, egg, minced onion, 3 tablespoons lemon juice, garlic, cumin, ½ teaspoon salt and red pepper in food processor or blender; process until well blended. Shape mixture into 1-inch balls; spray with nonstick cooking spray.
3. Preheat air fryer to 390°F. Line basket with foil; spray with cooking spray.
4. Cook in batches 12 to 15 minutes or until browned, turning halfway through cooking. Serve with sauce.

Potato Skins

MAKES 3 SERVINGS

- 3 small baking or red skinned potatoes, baked*
- 1 tablespoon butter, melted
- 1 teaspoon salt
- ⅛ teaspoon black pepper
- ½ cup (2 ounces) shredded Cheddar cheese
- 3 slices bacon, crisp-cooked and coarsely chopped
- ¼ cup sour cream
- 1 tablespoon snipped fresh chives

**Pierce potatoes with knife; bake in 425°F oven 45 minutes or in microwave on HIGH 5 minutes. Cool.*

1. Cut potatoes in half lengthwise. Scoop out soft middles leaving skins intact; reserve potato flesh for another use.
2. Brush potato skins with butter; sprinkle with salt and pepper.
3. Preheat air fryer to 370°F.
4. Cook potato skins 5 to 6 minutes or until crisp. Top with cheese and bacon; cook 3 to 5 minutes or until cheese is melted.
5. Cool slightly; top with sour cream and chives just before serving.

Buffalo Wings

MAKES 4 SERVINGS

- 1 cup hot pepper sauce
- ⅓ cup vegetable oil, plus additional for brushing
- 1 teaspoon sugar
- ½ teaspoon ground red pepper
- ½ teaspoon garlic powder
- ½ teaspoon Worcestershire sauce
- ⅛ teaspoon black pepper
- 1 pound chicken wings, tips removed, split at joints
- Blue cheese or ranch dressing
- Celery sticks (optional)

1. Combine hot pepper sauce, ⅓ cup oil, sugar, red pepper, garlic powder, Worcestershire sauce and black pepper in small saucepan; cook over medium heat 20 minutes. Remove from heat; pour sauce into large bowl.
2. Preheat air fryer to 370°F. Brush wings lightly with additional oil.
3. Cook wings in batches 16 to 18 minutes or until golden brown and cooked through, shaking halfway through cooking.
4. Transfer wings to bowl of sauce; stir to coat. Serve with blue cheese dressing and celery sticks, if desired.

Crispy Ravioli

MAKES 6 SERVINGS

- 1 cup all-purpose flour
- 2 eggs
- ¼ cup water
- 1 cup plain dry bread crumbs
- 1 teaspoon Italian seasoning
- ¾ teaspoon garlic powder
- ¼ teaspoon salt
- ½ cup grated Parmesan cheese
- 2 tablespoons finely chopped fresh parsley (optional)
- 1 package (10 ounces) cheese or meat ravioli, thawed if frozen
- ½ cup marinara sauce, warmed

1. Place flour in shallow dish. Beat eggs and water in another shallow dish. Combine bread crumbs, Italian seasoning, garlic powder and salt in third shallow dish. Combine cheese and parsley, if desired, in large bowl.
2. Coat ravioli with flour. Dip in egg mixture, letting excess drip back into dish. Roll in bread crumb mixture to coat. Spray with nonstick cooking spray.
3. Preheat air fryer to 390°F. Poke holes in ravioli with toothpick.
4. Cook ravioli in batches 5 to 6 minutes or until golden brown, turning halfway through cooking.
5. Add ravioli to bowl with cheese mixture; toss to coat. Serve warm with marinara sauce.

Mozzarella Sticks

MAKES 12 SERVINGS

- ¼ cup all-purpose flour
- 2 eggs
- 1 tablespoon water
- 1 cup plain dry bread crumbs
- 2 teaspoons Italian seasoning
- ½ teaspoon salt
- ½ teaspoon garlic powder
- 1 package (12 ounces) string cheese (12 sticks)
- 1 cup marinara or pizza sauce, warmed

1. Place flour in shallow dish. Beat eggs and water in another shallow dish. Combine bread crumbs, Italian seasoning, salt and garlic powder in third shallow dish.
2. Coat each piece of cheese with flour. Dip in egg mixture, letting excess drip back into dish. Roll in bread crumb mixture to coat. Dip again in egg mixture and roll again in bread crumb mixture. Place on baking sheet. Refrigerate until ready to cook.
3. Preheat air fryer to 370°F. Line basket with parchment paper; spray with nonstick cooking spray.
4. Cook cheese sticks in batches 8 to 10 minutes or until golden brown, turning halfway through cooking. Serve warm with marinara sauce.

MEAT

Renegade Steak

MAKES 2 SERVINGS

1½ teaspoons coarse salt
½ teaspoon paprika
½ teaspoon black pepper
¼ teaspoon onion powder
¼ teaspoon garlic powder
⅛ teaspoon turmeric
⅛ teaspoon ground red pepper
⅛ teaspoon ground coriander
2 center-cut sirloin, strip or tri-tip steaks (about 6 ounces each and 1 inch thick)
1 tablespoon butter, melted

1 Combine salt, paprika, black pepper, onion powder, garlic powder, turmeric, red pepper and coriander in small bowl; mix well. Season both sides of steaks with spice mixture (you will not need all of it); let steaks stand at room temperature 45 minutes before cooking.

2 Preheat air fryer to 390°F.

3 Cook steak 10 to 12 minutes or until desired doneness,* turning halfway through cooking.

4 Brush steaks with butter; cook 30 seconds. Remove steaks to plate; let stand 5 minutes before serving.

**Cook steaks to 130° to 135°F for medium rare or 140° to 145°F for medium.*

Pork with Spicy Orange Cranberry Sauce

MAKES 4 SERVINGS

- 1 teaspoon chili powder
- ½ teaspoon salt
- ½ teaspoon ground cumin
- ¼ teaspoon ground allspice
- ¼ teaspoon black pepper
- 4 boneless pork chops (about 4 ounces each and 1 inch thick)
- 1 tablespoon vegetable oil
- 1 cup whole berry cranberry sauce
- ½ teaspoon grated orange peel
- ¼ teaspoon ground cinnamon
- ⅛ teaspoon red pepper flakes

1. Combine chili powder, salt, cumin, allspice and black pepper in small bowl; mix well.
2. Pat pork chops dry with paper towels. Drizzle with oil; sprinkle both sides of pork with spice mixture, coating evenly.
3. Preheat air fryer to 380°F. Spray basket with nonstick cooking spray.
4. Cook pork chops in single layer 5 minutes; turn and cook 4 minutes or until pork is 145°F and barely pink in center.
5. Meanwhile, combine cranberry sauce, orange peel, cinnamon and red pepper flakes in small bowl; mix well. Serve sauce with pork chops.

Steak Fajitas

MAKES 2 SERVINGS

¼ cup lime juice
¼ cup soy sauce
2 tablespoons vegetable oil
2 tablespoons honey
2 tablespoons Worcestershire sauce
2 cloves garlic, minced
½ teaspoon ground red pepper
1 pound flank steak, skirt steak or top sirloin
1 medium yellow onion, halved and cut into ¼-inch slices
1 green bell pepper, cut into ¼-inch strips
1 red bell pepper, cut into ¼-inch strips
Flour tortillas, warmed
Lime wedges (optional)
Optional toppings: pico de gallo, guacamole, sour cream, shredded lettuce and shredded Cheddar-Jack cheese

1 Combine lime juice, soy sauce, oil, honey, Worcestershire sauce, garlic and ground red pepper in medium bowl; mix well. Remove ¼ cup marinade to large bowl. Place steak in large resealable food storage bag. Pour remaining marinade over steak; seal bag and turn to coat. Marinate in refrigerator at least 2 hours or overnight. Add onion and bell peppers to bowl with ¼ cup marinade; toss to coat. Cover and refrigerate until ready to use.

2 Remove steak from marinade; discard marinade. Pat steak dry with paper towels. Preheat air fryer to 390°F. Spray basket with nonstick cooking spray.

3 Cook steak 10 to 12 minutes or until desired doneness,* turning after 7 minutes. Remove to cutting board; tent with foil and let stand 10 minutes.

4 Add vegetable mixture** to air fryer; cook 8 to 10 minutes or until vegetables are crisp-tender and begin to brown in spots, shaking occasionally during cooking.

5 Cut steak into thin slices across the grain. Serve with vegetables, tortillas, lime wedges and desired toppings.

**Cook steak to 130° to 135°F for medium rare or 140° to 145°F for medium.*

***If your air fryer is small, you may need to cut steak in half and cook steak and vegetables in batches.*

Chorizo Quesadillas

MAKES 6 SERVINGS

- 1 package (9 ounces) uncooked Mexican chorizo sausage, casings removed
- 1 cup coarsely chopped cauliflower
- 1 small onion, finely chopped
- 12 (6-inch) flour tortillas
- 1½ cups (6 ounces) grated chihuahua cheese
- Salsa, guacamole and sour cream (optional)

1. Heat medium skillet over medium-high heat. Add chorizo, cauliflower and onion; cook and stir 10 to 12 minutes or until cauliflower is tender.
2. Place six tortillas on work surface. Spread ¼ cup chorizo mixture over each tortilla; top with ¼ cup cheese and remaining tortillas.
3. Preheat air fryer to 350°F. Spray basket with nonstick cooking spray.
4. Place one quesadilla in basket; spray with nonstick cooking spray. Place metal trivet, measuring cup or dinner knife on top of quesadilla (to prevent top tortilla from blowing off).
5. Cook quesadilla 4 minutes; turn and cook 2 to 3 minutes or until lightly browned. Repeat with remaining quesadillas. Cut into wedges; serve with salsa, guacamole and sour cream, if desired.

TIP: To keep cooked quesadillas warm, arrange on a baking sheet and place in a preheated 200°F oven until all the quesadillas are cooked and ready to serve.

Chicken Air-Fried Steak

MAKES 4 TO 6 SERVINGS

- ½ cup all-purpose flour
- ½ teaspoon salt
- ½ teaspoon onion powder
- ¼ teaspoon paprika
- ¼ teaspoon ground red pepper
- ⅛ teaspoon black pepper
- 1 egg
- ¼ cup water
- 1 pound cube steak, cut into 4 pieces

GRAVY

- 1½ tablespoons butter
- 2 to 3 tablespoons all-purpose flour
- ¾ cup chicken broth
- ½ cup milk
- Salt and black pepper

1. Combine ½ cup flour, ½ teaspoon salt, onion powder, paprika, red pepper and ⅛ teaspoon black pepper in shallow dish. Beat egg and water in another shallow dish.
2. Coat steaks with flour mixture, then dip in egg mixture, letting excess drip back into dish. Dip again in flour mixture to coat. Spray generously with nonstick cooking spray.
3. Preheat air fryer to 370°F. Spray basket with cooking spray or line with parchment paper sprayed with cooking spray.
4. Cook steak in batches 12 to 14 minutes or until browned and no longer pink in center, turning halfway through cooking. Remove to plate; tent with foil to keep warm.
5. Meanwhile, for gravy, melt butter in small skillet over medium heat. Add 2 tablespoons flour, broth and milk; cook and stir until slightly thickened. If necessary, add additional 1 tablespoon flour to thicken. Season with salt and black pepper. Serve with steak.

Mushroom Cheesesteak Sandwiches

MAKES 4 SERVINGS

- 8 ounces mushrooms, cut into ½-inch slices
- 1 medium onion, cut into ½-inch slices
- 1 green bell pepper, cut into ½-inch slices
- 1½ tablespoons vegetable oil, divided
- 1½ teaspoons salt, divided
- ½ teaspoon garlic powder
- ½ teaspoon black pepper, divided
- 1 pound skirt or flank steak
- 4 French bread or hoagie rolls (about 8 inches), split
- 8 slices provolone cheese

1. Preheat air fryer to 400°F. Combine mushrooms, onion, bell pepper, 1 tablespoon oil, ¾ teaspoon salt, garlic powder and ¼ teaspoon black pepper in large bowl; toss to coat.
2. Cook vegetables 5 to 7 minutes or until crisp-tender and beginning to brown, shaking halfway through cooking.
3. Meanwhile, cut steak in half lengthwise, then cut crosswise (against the grain) into ¼-inch slices. Place in medium bowl. Drizzle with remaining ½ tablespoon oil and season with remaining ¾ teaspoon salt and ¼ teaspoon black pepper; toss to coat.
4. Return cooked vegetables to large bowl. Add steak to air fryer in single layer; cook 2 minutes or until edges are browned. Add steak to vegetables in bowl; stir to blend. Cover to keep warm.
5. Place rolls in air fryer, cut sides up; cook 1 minute or until bread is toasted.
6. Spoon one fourth of steak and vegetable mixture onto bottom half of each roll; top with two slices cheese and top half of roll.

Breaded Pork Cutlets with Tonkatsu Sauce

MAKES 4 SERVINGS

- Tonkatsu Sauce (recipe follows)
- ½ cup all-purpose flour
- 2 eggs
- 2 tablespoons water
- 1½ cups panko bread crumbs
- 1 pound pork tenderloin, cut into ½-inch-thick slices
- Hot cooked rice

1 Prepare Tonkatsu Sauce.

2 Place flour in shallow dish. Beat eggs and water in another shallow dish. Spread panko on medium plate. Dip each pork slice first in flour, then egg mixture, letting excess drip back into dish. Coat both sides with panko.

3 Preheat air fryer to 370°F.

4 Cook pork in single layer 12 to 15 minutes or until barely pink in center. Serve pork over rice; drizzle with sauce.

Tonkatsu Sauce

MAKES ABOUT ⅓ CUP

- ¼ cup ketchup
- 1 tablespoon soy sauce
- 2 teaspoons sugar
- 2 teaspoons mirin (Japanese sweet rice wine)
- 1 teaspoon Worcestershire sauce
- 1 clove garlic, minced
- ½ teaspoon grated fresh ginger

Combine ketchup, soy sauce, sugar, mirin, Worcestershire sauce, garlic and ginger in small bowl; mix well.

French Quarter Steaks

MAKES 2 SERVINGS

- ½ cup water
- 2 tablespoons Worcestershire sauce
- 2 tablespoons soy sauce
- 1 tablespoon chili powder
- 3 cloves garlic, minced, divided
- 2 teaspoons paprika
- 1½ teaspoons ground red pepper
- 1⅛ teaspoons black pepper, divided
- 1 teaspoon onion powder
- 2 top sirloin steaks (about 6 ounces each and 1 inch thick)
- 4 tablespoons (½ stick) butter, divided
- 1 large onion, cut into ¼-inch slices
- 8 ounces thickly sliced mushrooms (white and shiitake or all white)
- ¼ teaspoon plus ⅛ teaspoon salt, divided

1 Combine water, Worcestershire sauce, soy sauce, chili powder, 2 cloves garlic, paprika, red pepper, 1 teaspoon black pepper and onion powder in small bowl; mix well. Place steaks in large resealable food storage bag. Pour marinade over steaks; seal bag and turn to coat. Marinate in refrigerator 1 to 3 hours.

2 Remove steaks from marinade 30 minutes before cooking; discard marinade. Pat steaks dry with paper towels. Preheat air fryer to 390°F.

3 Melt 1 tablespoon butter. Combine onion, mushrooms; melted butter, ¼ teaspoon salt and remaining ⅛ teaspoon black pepper in medium bowl; toss to coat. Cook 11 to 13 minutes or until vegetables are tender and edges begin to brown, shaking occasionally during cooking. Return to medium bowl; cover to keep warm.

4 Combine remaining 3 tablespoons butter, 1 clove garlic and ⅛ teaspoon salt in small skillet; cook over medium-low heat 3 minutes or until garlic begins to sizzle. Drizzle 1 tablespoon garlic butter over vegetables; toss to coat.

5 Cook steaks 10 to 15 minutes or until desired doneness,* turning halfway through cooking. Brush both sides of steaks with remaining garlic butter during last 2 minutes of cooking. Remove to plate and tent with foil; let stand 5 minutes. Serve steaks with vegetables.

**Cook steaks to 130° to 135°F for medium rare or 140° to 145°F for medium.*

California BBQ Burgers

MAKES 4 SERVINGS

- 4 tablespoons barbecue sauce, divided
- 2 tablespoons mayonnaise
- 1 medium onion, divided
- 1 pound ground beef
- 2 teaspoons olive oil
- ½ teaspoon salt
- ¼ teaspoon black pepper
- 4 burger buns, split and toasted
- 1 ripe avocado, sliced

1 Combine 2 tablespoons barbecue sauce and mayonnaise in small bowl; set aside. Cut ½ inch off top of onion; finely chop. (You should have about 1½ tablespoons.) Cut remaining onion into ¼-inch slices.

2 Combine beef, chopped onion and 1 tablespoon barbecue sauce in medium bowl; mix gently. Shape into four patties (about ½ inch thick); press indentation into center of each patty with thumb or fingertips.

3 Preheat air fryer to 360°F. Combine sliced onion and oil in small bowl stir to coat. Cook onion 4 minutes or until softened and beginning to brown, shaking halfway through cooking. Return onion to small bowl; stir in remaining 1 tablespoon barbecue sauce.

4 Season both sides of patties with salt and pepper; place in single layer in basket. Cook 5 minutes; turn and cook 2 to 3 minutes or until desired doneness (140 to 145°F for medium).

5 Spread 1 tablespoon mayonnaise mixture on top half of each bun. Place burgers on bottom halves of buns; top with cooked onions, avocado and top halves of buns.

Flank Steak with Italian Salsa

MAKES 6 SERVINGS

- 2 tablespoons olive oil
- 2 teaspoons balsamic vinegar
- 1 flank steak (about 1½ pounds)
- 1 tablespoon minced garlic
- ¾ teaspoon salt, divided
- ¾ teaspoon black pepper, divided
- 1 cup diced plum tomatoes
- ⅓ cup chopped pitted Kalamata olives
- 2 tablespoons chopped fresh basil

1 Whisk oil and vinegar in medium bowl until well blended. Place steak in shallow dish. Spread garlic over steak; sprinkle with ½ teaspoon salt and ½ teaspoon pepper. Spoon 2 tablespoons oil mixture over steak. Marinate in refrigerator at least 20 minutes or up to 2 hours.

2 Add tomatoes, olives, basil, remaining ¼ teaspoon salt and ¼ teaspoon pepper to remaining vinegar mixture in bowl; stir to coat.

3 Preheat air fryer to 400°F. Remove steak from marinade; discard marinade. (Leave garlic on steak.)

4 Cook steak 6 minutes; turn and cook about 6 minutes for medium rare (130° to 135°F) or until desired donenss. Remove to cutting board; tent with foil and let stand 5 minutes.

5 Cut steak diagonally across the grain into thin slices. Serve with tomato mixture.

Roasted Sausage with White Beans

MAKES 4 SERVINGS

- 1 pound uncooked mild or hot Italian sausage (4 links)
- 2 tablespoons extra virgin olive oil
- 10 fresh sage leaves (about 1 sprig)
- 2 cloves garlic, minced
- 1 can (about 14 ounces) diced tomatoes
- 2 cans (about 15 ounces each) cannellini beans, rinsed and drained
- ¼ teaspoon salt
- ⅛ teaspoon black pepper

1. Preheat air fryer to 360°F.
2. Cook sausages in single layer 6 minutes; turn and cook about 6 minutes or until browned and cooked through.
3. Meanwhile, heat oil in large skillet over medium-low heat. Add sage and garlic; cook 2 to 3 minutes or just until garlic begins to turn golden. Add tomatoes; bring to a simmer, stirring frequently.
4. Stir in beans, salt and pepper; cook 15 minutes, stirring occasionally. Serve sausages over beans.

Steak and Mushroom Supper

MAKES 4 SERVINGS

- 12 ounces boneless steak, cut into 1-inch pieces
- 8 ounces sliced mushrooms
- 1 onion, chopped
- 3 tablespoons melted butter, divided
- 1 teaspoon Worcestershire sauce
- ½ teaspoon garlic powder
- ½ teaspoon salt
- ¼ teaspoon black pepper
- Hot cooked egg noodles or rice (optional)
- Chopped fresh parsley

1. Combine steak, mushrooms and onion in large bowl. Add 1½ tablespoons butter, Worcestershire sauce and garlic powder; toss to coat.
2. Preheat air fryer to 390°F. Line basket with foil.
3. Cook steak mixture 10 to 12 minutes or until steak is cooked to desired donenss, shaking occasionally during cooking.
4. Transfer to large bowl. Add remaining 1½ tablespoons butter, salt and pepper; mix well. Serve over noodles, if desired; sprinkle with parsley.

Easy Beef Taquitos

MAKES 6 SERVINGS

- 12 ounces ground beef
- ¼ cup chopped onion
- 1 tablespoon taco seasoning mix
- 6 corn tortillas
- ⅓ cup shredded Cheddar cheese, plus additional for topping
- Salsa, sour cream and guacamole (optional)

1. Cook beef and onion in large skillet over medium-high heat 6 to 8 minutes or until browned, stirring to break up meat. Drain fat. Stir in taco seasoning mix; cook 2 minutes.
2. Spoon about 2 tablespoons beef mixture down center of each tortilla; top with 1 tablespoon cheese. Roll up tortillas to enclose filling; secure with toothpicks. Spray with nonstick cooking spray.
3. Preheat air fryer to 370°F.
4. Cook taquitos in single layer 3 to 4 minutes or until tortillas are browned and crisp.
5. Remove toothpicks before serving. Top with salsa, sour cream, guacamole and/or additional cheese, if desired.

VARIATION: Substitute ground turkey, chicken or pork for the ground beef in the taquito filling, or use leftover chopped cooked meat.

Open-Faced Steak and Blue Cheese Sandwiches

MAKES 4 SERVINGS

- 4 boneless beef top loin (strip) or tenderloin steaks, about ¾ inch thick
- 2 teaspoons olive oil
- ¾ teaspoon salt
- ¼ teaspoon black pepper
- 4 slices ciabatta bread
- 8 thin slices blue cheese

1 Bring steaks to room temperature. Rub steaks with oil; season both sides with salt and pepper.

2 Preheat air fryer to 400°F.

3 Cook steaks 5 minutes; turn and cook 4 minutes for medium rare (130° to 135°F) or until desired doneness. Remove to cutting board; tent with foil and let stand 5 minutes before slicing.

4 Meanwhile, toast bread. Slice steak; season with additional salt. Place two slices cheese on each toast slice; top with steak. Serve immediately.

TIP: While steak is resting, cook thick slices of sweet onion in the air fryer. Brush with oil; sprinkle with salt and cook about 10 minutes or until softened and beginning to brown, turning halfway through cooking. Separate onion into rings after cooking.

POULTRY

Zesty Italian Chicken Nuggets

MAKES 4 SERVINGS

2 boneless skinless chicken breasts (4 to 6 ounces each)
¼ cup zesty Italian salad dressing
2 tablespoons honey
¾ teaspoon salt
¼ teaspoon black pepper

1 Cut chicken into 1-inch pieces. Place in large resealable food storage bag.

2 Whisk dressing, honey, salt and pepper in medium bowl until well blended. Pour over chicken; seal bag and turn to coat. Marinate in refrigerator 30 minutes to 1 hour.

3 Preheat air fryer to 370°F. Line basket with parchment paper. Remove chicken from marinade; discard marinade.

4 Cook chicken in batches 10 to 12 minutes or until cooked through, shaking halfway through cooking.

Mexican Turkey Quesadillas

MAKES 4 SERVINGS

- 8 (8-inch) flour tortillas
- 1 cup finely chopped cooked turkey or chicken
- ½ cup salsa, plus additional for serving
- 1 cup (4 ounces) shredded Cheddar cheese
- 2 tablespoons chopped fresh cilantro
- 1 tablespoon olive oil
- Sour cream (optional)

1. Place four tortillas on work surface; top with turkey, ½ cup salsa, cheese and cilantro. Top with remaining four tortillas.
2. Preheat air fryer to 350°F. Spray basket with nonstick cooking spray.
3. Place one quesadilla in basket; spray with cooking spray. Place metal trivet, measuring cup or dinner knife on top of quesadilla (to prevent top tortilla from blowing off).
4. Cook 4 minutes; turn and cook 2 to 3 minutes or until lightly browned. Repeat with remaining quesadillas. Cut into wedges; serve with additional salsa and sour cream, if desired.

Chicken Cheddar Burgers

MAKES 4 SERVINGS

- 1¼ pounds ground chicken or turkey
- 1 cup plain dry bread crumbs
- ½ cup diced red bell pepper
- ½ cup ground walnuts
- ¼ cup sliced green onions
- ¼ cup light beer
- 2 tablespoons lemon juice
- 2 tablespoons chopped fresh parsley
- 2 cloves garlic, minced
- 1 teaspoon salt
- ¼ teaspoon black pepper
- 4 slices white Cheddar cheese
- 4 whole wheat buns
- Dijon mustard and lettuce leaves

1 Combine chicken, bread crumbs, bell pepper, walnuts, green onions, beer, lemon juice, parsley, garlic, salt and black pepper in large bowl; mix lightly. Shape into four patties.

2 Preheat air fryer to 390°F. Spray basket with nonstick cooking spray.

3 Cook patties 12 to 14 minutes or until cooked through (165°F), turning halfway through cooking. Place cheese on patties; cook 1 minute or just until cheese begins to melt.

4 Serve burgers on buns with mustard and lettuce.

Bang Bang Chicken

MAKES 4 SERVINGS

CREAMY HOT SAUCE

½ cup mayonnaise
¼ cup sweet chili sauce
1½ teaspoons hot pepper sauce

CHICKEN

½ cup all-purpose flour
¾ cup panko bread crumbs
1 pound boneless skinless chicken breasts, cut into 1-inch pieces
Hot cooked rice (optional)
2 green onions, chopped

1 For sauce, combine mayonnaise, chili sauce and hot pepper sauce in medium bowl; mix well. Reserve half of sauce for serving; place remaining half in shallow dish.

2 Place flour in separate shallow dish. Place panko in third shallow dish.

3 Coat chicken with flour. Dip chicken in sauce mixture, turning to coat. Roll in panko to coat. Spray chicken with nonstick cooking spray.

4 Preheat air fryer to 390°F. Line basket with parchment paper.

5 Cook chicken in batches 10 to 12 minutes or until golden brown and cooked through, shaking halfway through cooking. Serve over rice, if desired. Drizzle with sauce; sprinkle with green onions.

Hot Sweet Mustard Chicken

MAKES 4 TO 6 SERVINGS

- **4 cups small pretzel twists**
- **8 boneless skinless chicken thighs* (about 2 pounds)**
- **½ teaspoon salt**
- **¼ teaspoon black pepper**
- **½ cup hot sweet mustard**

****Boneless skinless chicken breasts can also be used; reduce cooking time to 12 to 15 minutes.***

1 Place pretzels in large resealable food storage bag; seal bag and crush pretzels with rolling pin, meat mallet or heavy skillet. (Pretzels should yield about 2 cups crumbs.) Place pretzel crumbs in shallow dish.

2 Season chicken with salt and pepper; generously brush all sides of chicken with mustard. Roll chicken in pretzel crumbs to coat, gently pressing crumbs into mustard to adhere.

3 Preheat air fryer to 380°F. Line basket with parchment paper.

4 Place chicken in single layer in basket; spray with nonstick cooking spray.

5 Cook chicken 8 minutes; turn and spray with cooking spray. Cook 8 to 10 minutes or until chicken is cooked through.

Quick Chicken Flautas

MAKES 4 SERVINGS

2 cups shredded cooked chicken*

⅔ cup chunky salsa

8 (6-inch) flour tortillas

Sour cream and guacamole (optional)

*Use a supermarket rotisserie chicken for convenience; one chicken will yield about 4 cups shredded meat.

1 Combine chicken and salsa in medium bowl; mix well. Place one tortilla on work surface; spread heaping ¼ cup chicken mixture on bottom half of tortilla. Roll up tightly into cylinder; secure with toothpick. Repeat with remaining tortillas and filling.

2 Preheat air fryer to 360°F. Spray basket with nonstick cooking spray.

3 Place half of tortilla rolls in basket seam side down; spray with cooking spray.

4 Cook 4 minutes; spray with cooking spray. Cook 2 to 3 minutes or until lightly browned. Repeat with remaining tortilla rolls.

5 Remove toothpicks; serve immediately with sour cream and guacamole, if desired.

Buttermilk Air-Fried Chicken

MAKES 4 SERVINGS

- **1 cut-up whole chicken (about 3 pounds)**
- **1 cup buttermilk**
- **¾ cup all-purpose flour**
- **½ teaspoon salt**
- **½ teaspoon ground red pepper**
- **¼ teaspoon garlic powder**
- **2 cups plain dry bread crumbs**

1. Place chicken pieces in large resealable food storage bag. Pour buttermilk over chicken; seal bag and turn to coat. Marinate in refrigerator at least 2 hours.
2. Combine flour, salt, red pepper and garlic powder in large shallow dish. Place bread crumbs in another shallow dish.
3. Preheat air fryer to 370°F. Spray basket with nonstick cooking spray.
4. Working with one piece at a time, remove chicken from bag. (Discard buttermilk.) Coat chicken with flour mixture, then roll in bread crumbs to coat. Spray with cooking spray.
5. Cook chicken in batches 20 to 25 minutes or until golden brown, crisp and cooked through (165°F).

Turkey Tostadas

MAKES 6 SERVINGS

- 1 pound ground turkey
- 1 package (1 ounce) taco seasoning
- ½ cup water
- 6 (6-inch) flour or corn tortillas
- 1 cup refried beans, warmed
- 1 cup shredded lettuce
- 1 large tomato, chopped
- 1 cup (4 ounces) shredded Mexican cheese blend
- 1 avocado, peeled and chopped
- 3 tablespoons sliced green onions
- ⅓ cup sour cream

1 Cook turkey in medium skillet over medium heat 6 to 8 minutes or until browned, stirring to break up meat. Stir in taco seasoning until well blended. Add water; cook 5 to 7 minutes or until water is absorbed, stirring occasionally.

2 Meanwhile, preheat air fryer to 400°F. Spray both sides of tortillas with nonstick cooking spray.

3 Place tortillas in single layer in basket (cook one or two tortillas at a time as space in your air fryer allows). Weigh down tortillas with trivet, metal measuring cup or ramekin to prevent them from blowing around.

4 Cook 2 minutes; turn and cook 2 to 3 minutes or until tortillas are golden brown and crisp.

5 Spread refried beans evenly over tortillas; top with turkey mixture, lettuce, tomato, cheese, avocado and green onions. Serve with sour cream.

Blue Cheese Stuffed Chicken Breasts

MAKES 4 SERVINGS

- ½ cup crumbled blue cheese
- 2 tablespoons butter, softened, divided
- ¾ teaspoon dried thyme
- Salt and black pepper
- 4 bone-in skin-on chicken breasts
- 1 tablespoon lemon juice

1 Combine blue cheese, 1 tablespoon butter and thyme in small bowl; mix well. Season with salt and pepper.

2 Loosen chicken skin by pushing fingers between skin and meat, taking care not to tear skin. Spread cheese mixture under skin; massage skin to spread mixture evenly over each chicken breast.

3 Melt remaining 1 tablespoon butter in small bowl; stir in lemon juice until blended. Brush mixture over chicken; sprinkle with salt and pepper.

4 Preheat air fryer to 370°F.

5 Cook chicken 15 to 20 minutes or until cooked through (165°F).

Buffalo Chicken Wraps

MAKES 2 SERVINGS

- **2 boneless skinless chicken breasts (about 4 ounces each)**
- **4 tablespoons buffalo wing sauce, divided**
- **1 cup broccoli coleslaw mix**
- **1 tablespoon blue cheese dressing**
- **2 (8-inch) whole wheat tortillas, warmed**

1. Place chicken in large resealable food storage bag. Add 2 tablespoons buffalo sauce; seal bag and turn to coat. Marinate in refrigerator 15 minutes.
2. Preheat air fryer to 370°F.
3. Cook chicken 14 to 18 minutes or until no longer pink in center. Set aside to cool 5 minutes.
4. Slice chicken; combine with remaining 2 tablespoons buffalo sauce in medium bowl.
5. Combine coleslaw mix and blue cheese dressing in small bowl; mix well. Spoon chicken and coleslaw down center of tortillas; roll up to enclose filling. Cut in half diagonally.

TIP: If you don't like the spicy flavor of buffalo wing sauce, substitute your favorite barbecue sauce.

Lemon Chicken

MAKES 4 SERVINGS

- 1 egg yolk
- 2 teaspoons soy sauce
- 1½ cups panko bread crumbs
- ⅛ teaspoon salt
- ⅛ teaspoon ground red pepper (optional)
- ⅛ teaspoon black pepper
- 1 pound chicken tenders or 1 pound boneless skinless chicken breasts, cut into long 1-inch-thick strips
- 1 cup chicken broth
- 1 tablespoon cornstarch
- 1 teaspoon vegetable oil
- 1 clove garlic, minced
- Grated peel of 1 small lemon
- 1 teaspoon sugar
- 1½ to 2½ teaspoons lemon juice

1. Preheat air fryer to 400°F. Beat egg yolk and soy sauce in shallow dish. Combine panko, salt, red pepper, if desired, and black pepper in another shallow dish.
2. Dip chicken strips in egg mixture, then roll in panko mixture to coat.
3. Line basket with parchment paper. Place chicken in single layer in basket; spray with nonstick cooking spray.
4. Cook chicken in batches 10 to 12 minutes or until golden brown and cooked through, turning halfway through cooking. (Make sure there is space between tenders or chicken will not be crisp.)
5. Meanwhile, stir broth into cornstarch in small bowl until smooth. Heat oil in small saucepan over low heat. Add garlic; cook and stir 1 minute or until softened. Stir in lemon peel. Add cornstarch mixture and sugar; cook and stir over medium heat 2 minutes or until thickened. Stir in 1½ teaspoons lemon juice; taste and add additional lemon juice, if desired. Drizzle sauce over chicken.

Garlic Chicken with Roasted Vegetables

MAKES 4 SERVINGS

- **3 tablespoons olive oil, divided**
- **1 teaspoon salt**
- **1 teaspoon dried oregano**
- **1 teaspoon paprika**
- **½ teaspoon black pepper**
- **2 cloves garlic, minced**
- **4 boneless skinless chicken breasts (about 4 ounces each)**
- **2 cups Brussels sprouts, trimmed and halved**
- **2 small onions, cut into wedges**
- **1 cup frozen crinkle-cut carrots**

1 Combine 2 tablespoons oil, 1 teaspoon salt, oregano, paprika, ½ teaspoon pepper and garlic in small bowl; mix well. Brush over chicken.

2 Preheat air fryer to 370°F. Line basket with parchment paper.

3 Cook chicken 15 to 20 minutes or until browned and no longer pink in center. Remove to plate; tent with foil to keep warm. *Increase temperature of air fryer to 390°F.*

4 Combine Brussels sprouts, onions, carrots and remaining 1 tablespoon oil in medium bowl; toss to coat. Season with salt and pepper.

5 Cook vegetables in batches 6 to 8 minutes or until tender and lightly browned, shaking halfway through cooking.

Chicken Bacon Quesadillas

MAKES 4 SERVINGS

- 1 cup (4 ounces) shredded Colby-Jack cheese
- 4 (8-inch) flour tortillas
- 1 cup coarsely chopped cooked chicken
- 4 slices bacon, crisp-cooked and coarsely chopped*
- ½ cup pico de gallo, plus additional for serving
- 1 tablespoon vegetable oil
- Sour cream and guacamole (optional)

**Cook bacon in preheated 390°F air fryer 6 to 8 minutes or until crisp. Remove to paper towel-lined plate to drain.*

1. Sprinkle ¼ cup cheese over half of one tortilla. Top with ¼ cup chicken, one fourth of bacon and 2 tablespoons pico de gallo. Fold tortilla in half over filling. Repeat with remaining ingredients. Brush both sides of quesadillas lightly with oil.
2. Preheat air fryer to 370°F. Spray basket with nonstick cooking spray.
3. Place quesadillas in single layer in basket; top with trivet, metal measuring cup or dinner knife to prevent top tortilla from opening.
4. Cook quesadillas 3 to 4 minutes or until cheese is melted and tortillas are golden brown. Transfer to cutting board to cool slightly.
5. Cut quesadillas into wedges. Serve with additional pico de gallo, sour cream and guacamole, if desired.

Garlicky Air-Fried Chicken Thighs

MAKES 4 SERVINGS

- **1 egg**
- **2 tablespoons water**
- **1 cup plain dry bread crumbs**
- **1 teaspoon salt**
- **1 teaspoon garlic powder**
- **½ teaspoon black pepper**
- **¼ teaspoon ground red pepper**
- **8 bone-in chicken thighs (about 3 pounds), skin removed**

1 Beat egg and water in shallow dish. Combine bread crumbs, salt, garlic powder, black pepper and red pepper in another shallow dish.

2 Dip chicken in egg mixture, letting excess drip back into dish. Roll in bread crumb mixture to coat.

3 Preheat air fryer to 390°F. Spray chicken with nonstick cooking spray.

4 Cook chicken 20 to 22 minutes or until golden brown and cooked through (165°F).

VARIATIONS: Substitute seasoned bread crumbs for the plain bread crumbs, salt, garlic powder, black pepper and red pepper. Or substitute your favorite herbs and spices for the garlic powder and red pepper.

SEAFOOD

Soy Ginger Salmon

MAKES 2 SERVINGS

- Crispy Shallots (optional, recipe follows)
- ¼ cup reduced-sodium soy sauce
- 2 tablespoons packed brown sugar
- 1 tablespoon grated fresh ginger
- 1 tablespoon butter
- 1 teaspoon Dijon mustard
- 2 salmon fillets (about 4 ounces each)

1. Prepare Crispy Shallots, if desired.
2. Combine soy sauce, brown sugar and ginger in small saucepan; bring to a simmer over medium heat. Cook 5 minutes or until slightly reduced and thickened. Remove from heat. Add butter and mustard; stir until butter is melted and mixture is smooth.
3. Preheat air fryer to 390°F. Spray basket with nonstick cooking spray. Brush salmon with soy sauce mixture.
4. Cook salmon 5 minutes; brush with soy sauce mixture. Cook 3 to 5 minutes or until fish begins to flake when tested with fork. Sprinkle with shallots.

CRISPY SHALLOTS: Cut two shallots into thin (⅛-inch) slices; place in small bowl. Drizzle with ½ teaspoon vegetable oil; toss to coat and separate into rings. Cook in air fryer at 250°F for 10 minutes. Stir shallots; cook 10 minutes or until shallots are golden brown and crisp. Sprinkle lightly with salt.

Southern Crab Cakes with Rémoulade Sauce

MAKES 4 SERVINGS

- 10 ounces fresh lump crabmeat
- 1½ cups fresh white or sourdough bread crumbs, divided
- ¼ cup chopped green onions
- ½ cup mayonnaise, divided
- 1 egg white, lightly beaten
- 2 tablespoons coarse grain or spicy brown mustard, divided
- ¾ teaspoon hot pepper sauce, divided
- Lemon wedges (optional)

1. Pick out and discard any shell or cartilage from crabmeat. Combine crabmeat, ¾ cup bread crumbs and green onions in medium bowl. Add ¼ cup mayonnaise, egg white, 1 tablespoon mustard and ½ teaspoon hot pepper sauce; mix gently.
2. Place remaining ¾ cup bread crumbs in shallow dish. Using ¼ cup mixture per cake, shape into eight ½-inch-thick cakes. Roll crab cakes gently in bread crumbs to coat.
3. Preheat air fryer to 370°F. Line basket with parchment paper.
4. Cook crab cakes in batches 8 to 10 minutes or until golden brown, turning halfway through cooking.
5. Meanwhile, combine remaining ¼ cup mayonnaise, 1 tablespoon mustard and ¼ teaspoon hot pepper sauce in small bowl. Serve crab cakes with sauce and lemon wedges, if desired.

Simple Baked Cod

MAKES 4 SERVINGS

- 4 cod fillets (about 6 ounces each)
- ½ teaspoon salt
- ¼ teaspoon black pepper
- ¼ cup (½ stick) butter
- 1 teaspoon chopped fresh thyme
- 2 teaspoons grated lemon peel
- 3 tablespoons chopped fresh parsley

1. Preheat air fryer to 400°F. Spray basket with nonstick cooking spray.
2. Place fish in basket; sprinkle with salt and pepper.
3. Cook cod 10 to 12 minutes or until fish begins to flake when tested with fork.
4. Meanwhile, melt butter in small saucepan over medium heat. Stir in thyme and lemon peel; cook 1 minute. Remove from heat; stir in parsley. Spoon butter mixture over fish. Serve immediately.

Tuna Pies

MAKES 4 SERVINGS

- 1 package (8 ounces) refrigerated crescent dough sheet
- 1 can (about 5 ounces) water-packed tuna, drained
- 1 tablespoon mayonnaise
- ½ cup (2 ounces) shredded Cheddar cheese

1. Spray four ovenproof bowls or ramekins with nonstick cooking spray.
2. Roll out dough into 12×8-inch rectangle on lightly floured surface. Cut into four 6×4-inch rectangles. Press dough into bottoms and up sides of prepared bowls.
3. Combine tuna and mayonnaise in small bowl; mix gently. Spoon tuna mixture evenly over dough; sprinkle with cheese.
4. Preheat air fryer to 370°F.
5. Cook pies in batches 8 to 10 minutes or until crust is golden brown. Let cool slightly before serving.

VARIATIONS: Add vegetables such as chopped broccoli, celery or peas to the tuna mixture, or substitute mozzarella or Swiss cheese for the Cheddar.

Lemon-Pepper Shrimp with Garlic Spinach

MAKES 4 SERVINGS

2 tablespoons olive oil, divided
1 tablespoon lemon juice
½ teaspoon salt, divided
½ teaspoon black pepper
¼ teaspoon garlic powder
¼ teaspoon paprika
1 pound medium raw shrimp, peeled and deveined
2 cloves garlic, minced
8 ounces baby spinach (about 8 cups lightly packed)
¼ cup water
Lemon wedges (optional)

1 Whisk 1 tablespoon oil, lemon juice, ¼ teaspoon salt, pepper, garlic powder and paprika in medium bowl until well blended. Add shrimp; toss to coat.

2 Preheat air fryer to 390°F. Spray basket with nonstick cooking spray.

3 Cook shrimp 6 to 8 minutes or until pink and opaque, shaking halfway through cooking.

4 Meanwhile, heat remaining 1 tablespoon oil in large skillet over medium-high heat. Add garlic; cook and stir 30 seconds. Add spinach, water and remaining ¼ teaspoon salt; cook 3 to 4 minutes or until spinach is wilted, stirring frequently. Drain excess liquid from skillet.

5 Serve shrimp over spinach. Serve with lemon wedges, if desired.

Island Fish Tacos

MAKES 4 SERVINGS

COLESLAW

1 medium jicama (about 12 ounces), peeled and shredded
2 cups packaged coleslaw mix
3 tablespoons finely chopped fresh cilantro
¼ cup lime juice
¼ cup vegetable oil
3 tablespoons white vinegar
2 tablespoons mayonnaise
1 tablespoon honey
1 teaspoon salt

TACOS

1 to 1¼ pounds white fish such as tilapia or mahi mahi, cut into 3×1½-inch pieces
Salt and black pepper
12 (6-inch) taco-size tortillas, heated
2 cups salsa or pico de gallo
Guacamole (optional)
Lime wedges (optional)

1. For coleslaw, combine jicama, coleslaw mix and 3 tablespoons cilantro in medium bowl. Whisk lime juice, oil, vinegar, mayonnaise, honey and 1 teaspoon salt in small bowl until well blended. Pour over vegetable mixture; stir to coat. Let stand at least 15 minutes for flavors to blend.
2. For tacos, season both sides of fish with salt and pepper.
3. Preheat air fryer to 350°F. Spray basket with nonstick cooking spray.
4. Cook fish in batches 8 to 10 minutes or until opaque and fish begins to flake when tested with fork, shaking halfway through cooking.
5. Break fish into bite-size pieces. Serve in tortillas with coleslaw, salsa, guacamole and lime wedges, if desired.

Salmon Bites with Broccoli

MAKES 5 SERVINGS

- 2 eggs
- 1 cup plain dry bread crumbs
- ¾ teaspoon salt, divided
- 1 pound skinless salmon fillet, cut into 1-inch pieces
- 2 cups broccoli florets
- 1 tablespoon olive oil
- Sweet and sour sauce or favorite dipping sauce (optional)

1. Beat eggs in shallow dish. Combine bread crumbs and ½ teaspoon salt in another shallow dish. Dip salmon in eggs, letting excess drip back into dish. Roll in bread crumbs to coat. Place salmon on plate; spray lightly with nonstick cooking spray.
2. Preheat air fryer to 390°F. Spray basket with cooking spray.
3. Cook salmon in batches 4 minutes. Turn and spray with cooking spray; cook 3 to 4 minutes or until golden brown. Remove to plate; tent with foil to keep warm.
4. Meanwhile, place broccoli in large bowl; drizzle with oil and toss to coat. Sprinkle with remaining ¼ teaspoon salt.
5. Cook broccoli 6 to 8 minutes or until browned and crisp, shaking halfway through cooking. Serve salmon and broccoli with sweet and sour sauce, if desired.

VARIATION: Substitute garlic-herb or Italian-seasoned bread crumbs for plain.

Tuna Cakes with Creamy Cucumber Sauce

MAKES 5 SERVINGS

- ½ cup finely chopped cucumber
- 6 ounces plain yogurt or plain Greek yogurt
- 1½ teaspoons chopped fresh dill *or* ½ teaspoon dried dill weed
- 1 teaspoon lemon-pepper seasoning
- ½ teaspoon salt, divided
- ⅓ cup shredded carrots
- ¼ cup sliced green onions
- ¼ cup finely chopped celery
- ¼ cup mayonnaise
- 2 teaspoons spicy brown mustard
- 1 cup panko bread crumbs, divided
- 1 can (12 ounces) albacore tuna in water, drained
- Lemon wedges (optional)

1. For sauce, combine cucumber, yogurt, dill, lemon-pepper seasoning and ¼ teaspoon salt in small bowl; mix well. Cover and refrigerate until ready to serve.
2. Combine carrots, green onions, celery, mayonnaise, mustard and remaining ¼ teaspoon salt in medium bowl; mix well. Stir in ½ cup panko. Add tuna; stir gently until blended.
3. Place remaining ½ cup panko in shallow dish. Shape tuna mixture into five ½-inch-thick patties. Roll patties gently in panko to coat.
4. Preheat air fryer to 370°F. Spray basket with nonstick cooking spray.
5. Cook patties in single layer 6 to 8 minutes or until golden brown, turning halfway through cooking. Serve with sauce and lemon wedges, if desired.

Bourbon-Marinated Salmon

MAKES 4 SERVINGS

¼ cup packed brown sugar
¼ cup bourbon
¼ cup soy sauce
2 tablespoons lime juice
1 tablespoon grated fresh ginger
1 tablespoon minced garlic
¼ teaspoon black pepper
4 salmon fillets (about 4 ounces each)
2 tablespoons minced green onion

1 Combine brown sugar, bourbon, soy sauce, lime juice, ginger, garlic and pepper in medium bowl; mix well. Reserve ¼ cup mixture for serving; set aside.

2 Place salmon in large resealable food storage bag. Pour remaining marinade over salmon; seal bag and turn to coat. Marinate in refrigerator 2 to 4 hours, turning occasionally.

3 Preheat air fryer to 390°F. Remove salmon from marinade; discard marinade.

4 Cook salmon 8 to 10 minutes or until fish begins to flake when tested with fork. Brush with reserved marinade mixture; sprinkle with green onion.

Supersize Shrimp

MAKES 4 SERVINGS

- ½ cup plain dry bread crumbs
- ¼ cup grated Parmesan cheese
- ½ teaspoon paprika
- ½ teaspoon salt
- ⅛ teaspoon black pepper
- 2 tablespoons butter, melted
- 1 pound large raw shrimp, peeled and deveined
- ½ cup mayonnaise
- ½ cup ketchup
- 1 tablespoon sweet pickle relish

1. Combine bread crumbs, cheese, paprika, salt and pepper in large bowl. Add butter; mix well. Rinse shrimp under cold water; drain well. Add to bread crumb mixture; turn to coat.
2. Preheat air fryer to 390°F. Line basket with parchment paper; spray with nonstick cooking spray.
3. Cook shrimp in batches 5 to 7 minutes or until lightly browned and cooked through.
4. Meanwhile, combine mayonnaise, ketchup and pickle relish in small bowl; mix well. Serve sauce with shrimp.

Roasted Dill Scrod with Asparagus

MAKES 4 SERVINGS

- 1 teaspoon olive oil
- 1 bunch (12 ounces) asparagus spears, trimmed
- ¾ teaspoon salt, divided
- 1 tablespoon lemon juice
- 4 scrod or cod fillets (about 5 ounces each)
- 1 teaspoon dried dill weed
- ¼ teaspoon black pepper
- Paprika (optional)

1. Preheat air fryer to 390°F. Line basket with parchment paper.
2. Drizzle oil over asparagus; roll spears to coat lightly with oil. Sprinkle with ¼ teaspoon salt.
3. Cook asparagus 8 to 10 minutes or until tender, shaking halfway through cooking. Remove to plate; keep warm.
4. Drizzle lemon juice over scrod. Combine dill weed, remaining ½ teaspoon salt and pepper in small bowl; sprinkle over fish.
5. Cook scrod 10 to 12 minutes or until opaque in center and fish begins to flake when tested with fork. Sprinkle with paprika, if desired. Serve with asparagus.

Salmon-Potato Cakes with Mustard Tartar Sauce

MAKES 4 SERVINGS

- 3 small unpeeled red potatoes (about 8 ounces), halved
- 1 cup water
- ½ teaspoon salt, divided
- 1 cup flaked cooked salmon
- 2 green onions, chopped
- 1 egg white
- 2 tablespoons chopped fresh parsley, divided
- ½ teaspoon Cajun or Creole seasoning
- 1 tablespoon mayonnaise
- 1 tablespoon plain yogurt or sour cream
- 2 teaspoons coarse grain mustard
- 1 tablespoon chopped dill pickle
- 1 teaspoon lemon juice

1 Combine potatoes, water and ¼ teaspoon salt in medium saucepan; bring to a boil over high heat. Reduce heat to medium; cook about 15 minutes or until potatoes are tender. Drain potatoes; mash with fork, leaving chunky texture.

2 Combine mashed potatoes, salmon, green onions, egg white, 1 tablespoon parsley, Cajun seasoning and remaining ¼ teaspoon salt in medium bowl; mix well.

3 Preheat air fryer to 370°F. Gently shape salmon mixture into four patties; flatten slightly.

4 Cook patties in single layer 5 to 6 minutes or until browned and heated through, turning halfway through cooking.

5 Meanwhile, combine mayonnaise, yogurt, mustard, pickle, remaining 1 tablespoon parsley and lemon juice in small bowl; mix well. Serve with salmon-potato cakes.

VEGETARIAN ENTRÉES

Caprese Portobellos

MAKES 4 SERVINGS

- 2 tablespoons butter
- 1 teaspoon dried parsley flakes
- ½ teaspoon minced garlic
- ¼ teaspoon salt
- 4 portobello mushrooms, cleaned and stemmed
- 1 cup (4 ounces) shredded mozzarella cheese
- 1 cup cherry or grape tomatoes, thinly sliced
- 2 tablespoons thinly sliced fresh basil
- Balsamic glaze

1. Combine butter, parsley flakes, garlic and salt in small microwavable dish; microwave on LOW (30%) 30 seconds or until butter is melted.
2. Preheat air fryer to 390°F. Spray basket with nonstick cooking spray.
3. Brush both sides of mushrooms with butter mixture. Fill each mushroom cap with about ¼ cup cheese; top with tomatoes.
4. Cook mushrooms 5 to 7 minutes or until cheese is melted and lightly browned. Top with basil.
5. Drizzle with balsamic glaze just before serving.

Hearty Veggie Sandwich

MAKES 4 SERVINGS

- 1 pound cremini mushrooms, stemmed and thinly sliced (⅛-inch slices)
- 2 teapoons olive oil, divided
- ¾ teaspoon salt, divided
- ¼ teaspoon black pepper
- 1 medium zucchini, diced (¼-inch pieces, about 2 cups)
- 3 tablespoons butter, softened
- 8 slices artisan whole grain bread
- ¼ cup pesto sauce
- ¼ cup mayonnaise
- 2 cups packed baby spinach
- 4 slices (1 ounce each) mozzarella cheese

1. Preheat air fryer to 370°F.
2. Combine mushrooms, 1 teaspoon oil, ½ teaspoon salt and pepper in medium bowl; toss to coat. Cook 6 to 8 minutes or until mushrooms are dark brown and dry, shaking occasionally during cooking. Return to medium bowl.
3. Combine zucchini, remaining 1 teaspoon oil and ¼ teaspoon salt in small bowl; toss to coat. Cook 2 to 4 minutes or until zucchini is tender and lightly browned. Return to small bowl.
4. Spread butter on one side of each bread slice. Turn over slices. Spread pesto on four bread slices; spread mayonnaise on remaining four slices. Top pesto-covered slices evenly with mushrooms; layer with spinach, zucchini and cheese. Top with remaining bread slices, mayonnaise side down.
5. Cook sandwiches 2 to 4 minutes or until bread is toasted, spinach is slightly wilted and cheese begins to melt. Serve immediately.

Fried Tofu with Asian Vegetables

MAKES 6 SERVINGS

- 1 pound firm tofu
- 4 tablespoons soy sauce, divided
- 1 cup all-purpose flour
- ⅛ teaspoon black pepper
- 1 package (16 ounces) frozen mixed Asian vegetables*
- 3 tablespoons water
- 1 teaspoon cornstarch
- 3 tablespoons plum sauce
- 2 tablespoons lemon juice
- 2 teaspoons sugar
- 1 teaspoon minced fresh ginger
- ⅛ to ¼ teaspoon red pepper flakes

***Frozen vegetables do not need to be thawed before cooking.**

1 Drain tofu; cut into ¾-inch cubes. Combine tofu and 2 tablespoons soy sauce in shallow dish; stir gently to coat. Let stand 5 minutes.

2 Combine flour and black pepper in another shallow dish. Gently toss tofu cubes, a small amount at a time, with flour mixture to coat. Spray tofu with nonstick cooking spray.

3 Preheat air fryer to 390°F. Cook tofu in batches 3 to 4 minutes or until browned. Remove to plate; keep warm.

4 Place frozen vegetables in basket. Cook 3 to 4 minutes or until vegetables are heated through, shaking halfway through cooking. Transfer to large bowl; cover to keep warm.

5 Stir water into cornstarch in small bowl until well blended. Combine cornstarch mixture, remaining 2 tablespoons soy sauce, plum sauce, lemon juice, sugar, ginger and red pepper flakes in medium microwavable bowl; cover and microwave on HIGH 1 minute or until sauce is slightly thickened, stirring after 30 seconds.

6 Add sauce and tofu to vegetables; toss gently to coat.

Eggplant Pizzas

MAKES 4 SERVINGS

- 1 egg
- 1 tablespoon water
- ¾ cup Italian-seasoned dry bread crumbs
- 1 medium eggplant, cut crosswise into ½-inch slices
- ½ cup marinara sauce
- ½ cup (2 ounces) shredded mozzarella cheese
- Chopped fresh basil

1. Beat egg and water in shallow dish. Place bread crumbs in another shallow dish. Dip eggplant slices in egg mixture, letting excess drip back into dish. Coat with bread crumbs, pressing gently to adhere. Spray with nonstick cooking spray.
2. Preheat air fryer to 370°F. Line basket with foil; spray foil with nonstick cooking spray.
3. Cook eggplant in batches 10 to 12 minutes or until slightly tender and golden brown, turning halfway through cooking.
4. Top each eggplant slice with 1 tablespoon marinara sauce and 1 tablespoon cheese. Cook 3 to 5 minutes or until cheese is melted and beginning to brown. Sprinkle with basil just before serving.

TIP: Add chopped bell peppers, sliced tomatoes, olives or other favorite pizza toppings; sprinkle over the marinara sauce, then top with cheese.

Black Bean and Rice Stuffed Poblano Peppers

MAKES 4 SERVINGS

- 4 poblano peppers
- 1 can (about 15 ounces) black beans, rinsed and drained
- 1 cup cooked brown rice
- ¾ cup (3 ounces) shredded Cheddar or pepper Jack cheese, divided
- ⅔ cup chunky salsa
- ¼ teaspoon salt

1. Cut thin slice from one side of each pepper; remove seeds and membranes. Chop pepper slices; set aside.
2. Preheat air fryer to 380°F. Spray peppers with nonstick cooking spray.
3. Cook peppers in single layer 6 to 8 minutes or until skin is slightly softened. Remove to plate. *Reduce temperature of air fryer to 350°F.*
4. Combine beans, rice, ½ cup cheese, salsa, chopped poblano pepper and salt in medium bowl; mix well. Spoon mixture evenly into peppers, mounding in center. Line air fryer basket with parchment paper; place filled peppers in air fryer basket. (Make sure there is space between peppers for air circulation, or cook in two batches.)
5. Cook peppers 6 to 8 minutes or until heated through. Sprinkle with remaining ¼ cup cheese; cook 2 minutes or until cheese is melted.

TIP: Use a package of cooked brown rice for the filling to save time.

Cauliflower Tacos with Chipotle Crema

MAKES 8 TACOS

- 1 package (8 ounces) sliced cremini mushrooms
- 4 tablespoons olive oil, divided
- ¼ teaspoon salt
- 1 head cauliflower, florets cut into 1-inch pieces
- 1 teaspoon ground cumin
- ½ teaspoon dried oregano
- ¼ teaspoon ground coriander
- ¼ teaspoon ground cinnamon
- ¼ teaspoon black pepper
- ½ cup sour cream
- 2 teaspoons lime juice
- ½ teaspoon chipotle chili powder
- ½ cup vegetarian refried beans
- 8 (6-inch) corn or flour tortillas
- Chopped fresh cilantro (optional)
- Pickled Red Onions (recipe follows) or chopped red onion

1. Combine mushrooms, 1 tablespoon oil and salt in medium bowl; toss to coat.
2. Place cauliflower in large bowl. Add remaining 3 tablespoons oil, cumin, oregano, coriander, cinnamon and pepper; toss to coat.
3. Preheat air fryer to 390°F. Spray basket with nonstick cooking spray. Cook cauliflower in batches 8 to 10 minutes or until browned and tender, shaking occasionally during cooking. Return to large bowl.
4. Add mushrooms to basket. Cook 6 to 8 minutes or until browned, shaking occasionally during cooking.
5. Combine sour cream, lime juice and chili powder in small bowl; mix well.
6. For each taco, spread 1 tablespoon beans and 1 teaspoon sour cream mixture over tortilla; top with about 3 mushroom slices and ¼ cup cauliflower. Top with cilantro and pickled onions, if desired.

PICKLED RED ONIONS: Thinly slice 1 small red onion; place in large glass jar. Add ¼ cup distilled white vinegar, 2 tablespoons water, 1 teaspoon sugar and 1 teaspoon salt. Seal jar; shake well. Refrigerate at least 1 hour or up to 1 week.

Crustless Spinach Quiche

MAKES 6 SERVINGS

- 8 eggs
- 1 cup half-and-half
- 1 teaspoon Italian seasoning
- ¾ teaspoon salt
- ½ teaspoon black pepper
- 1 package (10 ounces) frozen chopped spinach, thawed and squeezed dry
- 1¼ cups (5 ounces) shredded Italian cheese blend

1. Preheat air fryer to 330°F. Line 8-inch round baking pan* with parchment paper; spray with nonstick cooking spray.
2. Beat eggs, half-and-half, Italian seasoning, salt and pepper in medium bowl until well blended. Stir in spinach and cheese; mix well. Pour into prepared pan.
3. Cook 30 minutes or until toothpick inserted into center comes out clean. Cover with foil if top is browning too much. Remove to wire rack to cool 10 minutes.
4. To remove quiche from pan, run knife around edge of pan to loosen. Invert quiche onto plate and remove parchment paper; invert again onto cutting board or serving plate. Cut into wedges.

**If 8-inch pan doesn't fit in your air fryer, use two smaller baking pans, reduce cooking time and cook in two batches.*

Tuscan Portobello Melt

MAKES 2 SERVINGS

- 1 portobello mushroom cap, thinly sliced
- ½ small red onion, thinly sliced
- ½ cup grape tomatoes
- 1 tablespoon olive oil
- 1 teaspoon balsamic vinegar
- ⅛ teaspoon salt
- ⅛ teaspoon dried thyme
- ⅛ teaspoon black pepper
- 2 tablespoons butter, softened, divided
- 4 slices sourdough bread
- 2 slices provolone cheese
- 2 teaspoons Dijon mustard
- 2 slices Monterey Jack cheese

1. Combine mushroom, onion and tomatoes in small bowl. Drizzle with oil and vinegar; sprinkle with salt, thyme and pepper and toss to coat.
2. Preheat air fryer to 390°F. Spray basket with nonstick cooking spray.
3. Cook vegetables 8 to 10 minutes or until tender, shaking occasionally during cooking.
4. Spread half of butter over one side of bread slices. Cook bread 2 to 4 minutes or until golden brown. Transfer bread to cutting board, buttered sides up.
5. Place provolone on two bread slices; spread mustard over cheese. Top with vegetables, Monterey Jack and remaining bread slices, buttered sides down. Spread remaining butter over outsides of sandwiches.
6. Cook sandwiches 1 to 2 minutes or until cheese is melted.

Fried Tofu with Sesame Dipping Sauce

MAKES 4 SERVINGS

- 3 tablespoons soy sauce or tamari
- 2 tablespoons unseasoned rice vinegar
- 2 teaspoons sugar
- 1 teaspoon sesame seeds, toasted*
- 1 teaspoon dark sesame oil
- ⅛ teaspoon red pepper flakes
- 1 package (about 14 ounces) extra firm tofu
- ¼ cup all-purpose flour
- 1 egg
- 1 cup panko bread crumbs
- Salt

**To toast sesame seeds, spread seeds in small skillet. Shake skillet over medium-low heat about 3 minutes or until seeds begin to pop and turn golden.*

1. Whisk soy sauce, vinegar, sugar, sesame seeds, sesame oil and red pepper flakes in small bowl until well blended; set aside.
2. Drain tofu and press between paper towels to remove excess water. Cut crosswise into four slices; cut each slice diagonally into triangles.
3. Place flour in shallow dish. Beat egg in another shallow dish. Place panko in third shallow dish.
4. Dip each piece of tofu in flour, turning to lightly coat all sides. Dip in egg, letting excess drip back into dish. Roll in panko to coat. Season with salt.
5. Preheat air fryer to 390°F. Spray tofu with nonstick cooking spray.
6. Cook tofu in batches 5 to 6 minutes or until golden brown, turning halfway through cooking. Serve with sauce for dipping.

Southwestern Black Bean and Corn Flatbread

MAKES 4 SERVINGS

- 1 can (about 15 ounces) black beans, rinsed and drained
- 1 cup frozen corn, thawed
- ½ cup finely chopped red onion
- 1 teaspoon olive oil
- ½ teaspoon salt
- ¼ cup green chile enchilada sauce
- 2 oval flatbreads (about 11×7 inches)
- 2 cups (8 ounces) shredded Monterey Jack cheese
- 1 avocado, diced
- 2 tablespoons fresh chopped cilantro
- Lime wedges (optional)

1. Combine beans, corn, onion, oil and salt in medium bowl; mix well.
2. Spread enchilada sauce over flatbreads. Sprinkle with cheese; top with bean mixture.
3. Preheat air fryer to 400°F.
4. Cook flatbreads in single layer about 9 minutes or until cheese is melted and crusts are golden brown and crisp.
5. Sprinkle with avocado and cilantro; cut into halves or quarters. Serve with lime wedges, if desired.

Barbecue Cauliflower Calzones

MAKES 4 SERVINGS

- 1 head cauliflower, cut into florets and thinly sliced
- 2 tablespoons olive oil
- Salt and black pepper
- ¾ cup barbecue sauce, plus additional for serving
- 1 container (about 14 ounces) refrigerated pizza dough
- ½ onion, chopped
- 1 cup (4 ounces) shredded mozzarella cheese
- Ranch or blue cheese dressing (optional)

1. Preheat air fryer to 390°F.
2. Place cauliflower in medium bowl. Drizzle with oil and season lightly with salt and pepper; toss to coat.
3. Cook cauliflower 6 to 8 minutes or until slightly tender and lightly browned, shaking halfway through cooking. Return to medium bowl; stir in ¾ cup barbecue sauce. *Reduce temperature of air fryer to 370°F.*
4. Unroll pizza dough onto lightly floured cutting board. Stretch dough into 11×17-inch rectangle; cut into quarters. Place one fourth of onion on half of each piece of dough; top with one fourth of cauliflower and ¼ cup cheese. Fold dough over filling; roll and pinch edges to seal. Spray with nonstick cooking spray.
5. Cook calzones in batches 5 to 7 minutes or until golden brown. Serve with additional barbecue sauce and ranch dressing, if desired.

Spicy Eggplant Burgers

MAKES 4 SERVINGS

- 1 eggplant (about 1¼ pounds)
- 2 egg whites
- ½ cup Italian-style panko bread crumbs
- 3 tablespoons chipotle mayonnaise or regular mayonnaise
- 4 whole wheat hamburger buns, warmed
- 1½ cups loosely packed baby spinach
- 8 thin slices tomato
- 4 slices pepper Jack cheese

1. Cut four (½-inch-thick) slices from widest part of eggplant. Beat egg whites in shallow dish. Place panko in another shallow dish.
2. Dip eggplant slices in egg whites; coat with panko, pressing gently to adhere. Spray with nonstick cooking spray.
3. Preheat air fryer to 370°F. Line basket with foil; spray foil with nonstick cooking spray.
4. Cook eggplant in batches 8 to 10 minutes or until golden brown, turning halfway through cooking.
5. Spread mayonnaise on bottom halves of buns; top with spinach, tomato, eggplant, cheese and tops of buns.

SIDE DISHES

Cinnamon-Honey Glazed Carrot Chips

MAKES 6 SERVINGS

¼ cup honey
2 tablespoons butter
1 teaspoon ground cinnamon
½ teaspoon ground nutmeg
Pinch of salt
1 package (16 ounces) carrot chips or baby carrots

1 Combine honey and butter in medium microwavable bowl; microwave on HIGH 30 seconds until melted. Add cinnamon, nutmeg and salt; stir until blended.

2 Add carrots to honey mixture; toss to coat.

3 Preheat air fryer to 390°F. Line basket with parchment paper.

4 Cook carrots in batches 12 to 15 minutes or until browned and slightly tender, shaking occasionally during cooking.

Brussels Sprouts with Honey Butter

MAKES 4 SERVINGS

- 6 slices thick-cut bacon, cut into ½-inch pieces
- 1½ pounds Brussels sprouts (about 24 medium), halved
- ¼ teaspoon salt
- ¼ teaspoon black pepper
- 2 tablespoons butter, softened
- 2 tablespoons honey

1. Cook bacon in medium skillet until almost crisp. Drain on paper towel-lined plate; set aside.
2. Place Brussels sprouts in medium bowl. Pour 1 tablespoon bacon drippings over Brussels sprouts (discard remaining drippings). Sprinkle with ¼ teaspoon salt and ¼ teaspoon pepper; toss to coat.
3. Preheat air fryer to 370°F.
4. Cook Brussels sprouts in single layer 8 to 10 minutes or until browned, shaking occasionally during cooking.
5. Combine butter and honey in medium bowl; mix well. Add warm Brussels sprouts; stir until completely coated. Stir in bacon; season with additional salt and pepper.

Garlic Seasoned Mushrooms

MAKES 4 SERVINGS

- 1 pound mushrooms, trimmed and halved
- 2 tablespoons olive oil
- 1 teaspoon garlic powder
- 1 teaspoon Italian seasoning
- ½ teaspoon salt
- ¼ teaspoon black pepper
- Fresh chopped parsley (optional)
- Lemon wedges (optional)

1. Preheat air fryer to 370°F.
2. Combine mushrooms, oil, garlic powder, Italian seasoning, salt and pepper in large bowl; toss to coat.
3. Cook mushrooms 12 to 15 minutes or until tender and browned, shaking occasionally during cooking. Sprinkle with parsley; serve with lemon wedges, if desired.

Air-Fried Corn on the Cob

MAKES 2 SERVINGS

- **2 teaspoons butter, melted**
- **½ teaspoon chopped fresh parsley**
- **¼ teaspoon salt**
- **¼ teaspoon black pepper**
- **2 ears corn, husks and silks removed**
- **Foil**
- **Grated Parmesan cheese (optional)**

1. Combine butter, parsley, salt and pepper in small bowl; mix well. Brush corn with butter mixture.
2. Preheat air fryer to 390°F. Wrap each ear of corn in foil.*
3. Cook corn 6 to 8 minutes, turning halfway through cooking. Sprinkle with cheese, if desired.

**If your air fryer basket is too small to fit whole ears of corn, break them in half to fit.*

Italian-Style Roasted Vegetables

MAKES 6 SERVINGS

- 1 small eggplant, cut into chunks
- 1 small zucchini, cut into chunks
- 1 small red bell pepper, cut into chunks
- 1 small yellow bell pepper, cut into chunks
- 1 small onion, cut into chunks
- 10 cloves garlic
- 1 tablespoon olive oil
- 1 teaspoon white vinegar
- ½ teaspoon salt
- ½ teaspoon dried basil
- ½ teaspoon dried oregano
- ¼ teaspoon red pepper flakes
- Shredded Parmesan cheese (optional)

1. Combine eggplant, zucchini, bell peppers, onion and garlic in large bowl. Add oil, vinegar, salt, basil, oregano and red pepper flakes; toss to coat.
2. Preheat air fryer to 390°F. Spray basket with nonstick cooking spray.
3. Cook vegetables in batches 12 to 15 minutes or until tender and browned, shaking halfway through cooking.
4. Sprinkle with cheese, if desired.

Parmesan Fries with Rosemary Dipping Sauce

MAKES 4 SERVINGS

- 3 medium baking potatoes (about 8 ounces each), peeled and cut into 12 wedges
- 1 tablespoon olive oil
- ¼ teaspoon salt
- ⅛ teaspoon black pepper
- ¼ cup grated Parmesan cheese
- ½ cup mayonnaise
- 1 teaspoon chopped fresh rosemary *or* ½ teaspoon dried rosemary
- ½ teaspoon grated lemon peel
- 1 clove garlic, minced

1 Combine potatoes, oil, salt and pepper in medium bowl; toss to coat.

2 Preheat air fryer to 390°F.

3 Cook potatoes in batches 18 to 20 minutes or until almost tender, shaking halfway through cooking.

4 Sprinkle with cheese; cook 3 to 5 minutes or until cheese is melted and potatoes are tender and lightly browned.

5 Meanwhile, combine mayonnaise, rosemary, lemon peel and garlic in small bowl; mix well. Serve sauce with potatoes.

Air-Fried Green Beans

MAKES 4 SERVINGS

- 1 pound fresh green beans, trimmed
- 1 tablespoon olive oil
- ½ teaspoon salt
- ¼ teaspoon black pepper
- 1 lemon, cut into wedges
- 2 tablespoons grated Parmesan cheese

1. Preheat air fryer to 380°F.
2. Combine beans, oil, salt and pepper in large bowl; toss to coat.
3. Cook beans in two batches 8 to 10 minutes or until crisp-tender and lightly browned, shaking halfway through cooking.
4. Squeeze lemon wedges over beans; sprinkle with cheese.

Taco Roasted Cauliflower

MAKES 4 TO 6 SERVINGS

1 medium cauliflower (about 2 pounds), cut into florets
2 tablespoons vegetable oil
1 package (1 ounce) taco seasoning mix

1. Preheat air fryer to 370°F.
2. Place cauliflower in large bowl. Drizzle with oil and sprinkle with seasoning mix; toss to coat.
3. Cook cauliflower 20 to 25 minutes or until tender and lightly browned, shaking twice during cooking.*

**Cooking the entire cauliflower in one batch will result in tender cauliflower that is less crisp. For crisper cauliflower, cook in single layer in several batches; reduce cooking time to 15 minutes and shake halfway through cooking.*

Thai Broccoli Salad

MAKES 4 TO 6 SERVINGS

- 6 cups fresh broccoli florets (1-inch pieces)
- 1 small red bell pepper, chopped (½-inch pieces)
- 2 tablespoons peanut or vegetable oil
- ¼ teaspoon salt
- 2 tablespoons peanut butter
- 1½ tablespoons hot water
- 1 tablespoon lime juice
- 1 tablespoon packed brown sugar
- 1 tablespoon soy sauce
- 2 teaspoons dark sesame oil
- 1 clove garlic, minced
- ¼ teaspoon red pepper flakes

1. Combine broccoli and bell pepper in large bowl. Drizzle with peanut oil and sprinkle with salt; toss to coat.
2. Preheat air fryer to 360°F.
3. Cook vegetables 15 minutes or until crisp-tender, shaking twice during cooking.
4. Meanwhile, whisk peanut butter, water, lime juice, brown sugar, soy sauce, sesame oil, garlic and red pepper flakes in same large bowl until smooth and well blended.
5. Add vegetables to peanut butter mixture; toss to coat. Serve warm or at room temperature.

Roasted Balsamic Asparagus

MAKES 4 SERVINGS

- 1 pound fresh asparagus
- 1 tablespoon olive oil
- ½ teaspoon salt
- ¼ teaspoon black pepper
- 1 tablespoon balsamic glaze*
- ¼ cup shredded or grated Parmesan cheese
- Grated lemon peel (optional)

**Balsamic glaze can be found in the condiment section of the supermarket or can be prepared by simmering 2 tablespoons balsamic vinegar until reduced by about half.*

1 Preheat air fryer to 400°F.

2 Place asparagus in shalllow dish. Drizzle with oil and season with salt and pepper; roll spears to coat.

3 Cook asparagus 6 to 8 minutes or until tender and beginning to brown, shaking halfway through cooking. Transfer to serving plate.

4 Drizzle asparagus with balsamic glaze; roll again with tongs to coat. Sprinkle with cheese; garnish with lemon peel.

Crispy Brussels Sprouts

MAKES 4 SERVINGS

- 1 pound Brussels sprouts, trimmed and halved
- ¼ cup ground almonds
- 2 tablespoons grated Parmesan cheese
- 1½ tablespoons olive oil
- 1 tablespoon everything bagel seasoning

1. Preheat air fryer to 370°F.
2. Combine Brussels sprouts, almonds, cheese, oil and bagel seasoning in medium bowl; toss to coat.
3. Cook Brussels sprouts in batches 8 to 10 minutes or until browned and crisp, shaking occasionally during cooking.

Roasted Sweet Potatoes and Onions

MAKES 4 SERVINGS

- 2 unpeeled sweet potatoes (about 1¼ pounds)
- 1 medium sweet or yellow onion, cut into chunks
- 2 tablespoons canola oil
- 1 teaspoon dried thyme
- ½ teaspoon salt
- ½ teaspoon smoked paprika
- ⅛ teaspoon ground red pepper (optional)

1 Cut sweet potatoes into 1-inch pieces; place in large bowl. Add onion, oil, thyme, salt, paprika and red pepper, if desired; toss to coat.

2 Preheat air fryer to 400°F. Spray basket with nonstick cooking spray.

3 Cook vegetables 20 to 25 minutes or until tender and beginning to brown, shaking halfway through cooking.

Roasted Cremini Mushrooms

MAKES 4 SERVINGS

- 1 pound cremini mushrooms, halved or quartered if large
- ½ cup sliced shallots
- 1 tablespoon olive oil
- ¾ teaspoon salt
- ½ teaspoon dried rosemary, crushed*
- ¼ teaspoon black pepper
- Fresh rosemary sprigs (optional)

***If the holes in your air fryer basket are large, much of the dried rosemary may fall through. Crushing the rosemary before tossing it with the vegetables will help prevent this from happening.**

1. Preheat air fryer to 370°F.
2. Combine mushrooms and shallots in medium bowl. Drizzle with oil; sprinkle with salt, dried rosemary and pepper and toss to coat.
3. Cook mushrooms 8 to 10 minutes or until tender and lightly browned, shaking twice during cooking. Garnish with fresh rosemary.

Mexican Corn Ribs

MAKES 4 SERVINGS

- 2 ears corn
- ¼ cup (½ stick) butter, softened
- ½ teaspoon chili powder
- ¼ teaspoon garlic powder
- ¼ teaspoon black pepper
- ¼ cup mayonnaise
- 2 teaspoons lime juice
- 1 teaspoon hot pepper sauce
- 2 tablespoons cotija or feta cheese
- 1 tablespoon chopped fresh cilantro

1. Husk corn and remove silk. Rinse and dry corn.
2. Use large knife to cut ears of corn in half horizontally, then cut each half lengthwise into quarters to create four "ribs."
3. Combine butter, chili powder, garlic powder and black pepper in small bowl; mix well. Spread mixture over corn.
4. Preheat air fryer to 390°F. Line basket with parchment paper.
5. Cook corn 12 to 14 minutes or until charred, turning halfway through cooking. Remove to plate.
6. Meanwhile, combine mayonnaise, lime juice and hot pepper sauce in small bowl; mix well. Brush over corn; sprinkle with cheese and cilantro.

Greek Lemon Potatoes

MAKES 4 SERVINGS

- 2½ pounds Yukon gold or yellow potatoes, peeled and cut into 1-inch pieces
- 3 tablespoons lemon juice, divided
- 2 tablespoons olive oil
- 2 teaspoons Greek seasoning
- Chopped fresh parsley (optional)

1 Preheat air fyer to 400°F. Combine potatoes, 2 tablespoons lemon juice, oil and Greek seasoning in medium bowl; toss to coat.

2 Cook potatoes in batches about 14 minutes or until tender and golden brown, shaking halfway through cooking.

3 Drizzle potatoes with remaining 1 tablespoon lemon juice; sprinkle with parsley, if desired. Serve immediately.

Glazed Maple Acorn Squash

MAKES 4 SERVINGS

1 large acorn squash
2 tablespoons butter, melted
2 tablespoons maple syrup
½ teaspoon salt
¼ teaspoon ground cinnamon
⅛ teaspoon black pepper

1 Preheat air fryer to 375°F. Spray basket with nonstick cooking spray.

2 Cut off stem and blossom ends of squash. Cut squash crosswise into four equal slices, discarding seeds and membrane. Combine butter, maple syrup, salt, cinnamon and pepper in small bowl; mix well.

3 Brush both sides of squash slices with butter mixture. (Reserve small amount for after cooking.)

4 Cook squash 20 minutes or until tender, turning halfway through cooking. Brush squash with remaining butter mixture immediately after cooking.

INDEX

INDEX

Metric Conversion Chart

VOLUME MEASUREMENTS (dry)

1/8 teaspoon = 0.5 mL
1/4 teaspoon = 1 mL
1/2 teaspoon = 2 mL
3/4 teaspoon = 4 mL
1 teaspoon = 5 mL
1 tablespoon = 15 mL
2 tablespoons = 30 mL
1/4 cup = 60 mL
1/3 cup = 75 mL
1/2 cup = 125 mL
2/3 cup = 150 mL
3/4 cup = 175 mL
1 cup = 250 mL
2 cups = 1 pint = 500 mL
3 cups = 750 mL
4 cups = 1 quart = 1 L

VOLUME MEASUREMENTS (fluid)

1 fluid ounce (2 tablespoons) = 30 mL
4 fluid ounces (1/2 cup) = 125 mL
8 fluid ounces (1 cup) = 250 mL
12 fluid ounces (1 1/2 cups) = 375 mL
16 fluid ounces (2 cups) = 500 mL

WEIGHTS (mass)

1/2 ounce = 15 g
1 ounce = 30 g
3 ounces = 90 g
4 ounces = 120 g
8 ounces = 225 g
10 ounces = 285 g
12 ounces = 360 g
16 ounces = 1 pound = 450 g

DIMENSIONS

1/16 inch = 2 mm
1/8 inch = 3 mm
1/4 inch = 6 mm
1/2 inch = 1.5 cm
3/4 inch = 2 cm
1 inch = 2.5 cm

OVEN TEMPERATURES

250°F = 120°C
275°F = 140°C
300°F = 150°C
325°F = 160°C
350°F = 180°C
375°F = 190°C
400°F = 200°C
425°F = 220°C
450°F = 230°C

BAKING PAN SIZES

Utensil	Size in Inches/Quarts	Metric Volume	Size in Centimeters
Baking or Cake Pan (square or rectangular)	8×8×2	2 L	20×20×5
	9×9×2	2.5 L	23×23×5
	12×8×2	3 L	30×20×5
	13×9×2	3.5 L	33×23×5
Loaf Pan	8×4×3	1.5 L	20×10×7
	9×5×3	2 L	23×13×7
Round Layer Cake Pan	8×1½	1.2 L	20×4
	9×1½	1.5 L	23×4
Pie Plate	8×1¼	750 mL	20×3
	9×1¼	1 L	23×3
Baking Dish or Casserole	1 quart	1 L	—
	1½ quart	1.5 L	—
	2 quart	2 L	—